Searching for Tara

The Goddess Who Became a Buddha

James William Coleman

BLOOMSBURY ACADEMIC
NEW YORK • LONDON • OXFORD • NEW DELHI • SYDNEY

BLOOMSBURY ACADEMIC
Bloomsbury Publishing Inc, 1359 Broadway, New York, NY 10018, USA
Bloomsbury Publishing Plc, 50 Bedford Square, London, WC1B 3DP, UK
Bloomsbury Publishing Ireland, 29 Earlsfort Terrace, Dublin 2, D02 AY28, Ireland

BLOOMSBURY, BLOOMSBURY ACADEMIC and the Diana logo are trademarks of Bloomsbury Publishing Plc

First published in the United States of America 2027

Cover design: Diana Nuhn
Cover image courtesy of the Garchen Buddhist Institute

A catalog record for this book is available from the Library of Congress.

ISBN: HB: 979-8-216-38126-6
PB: 979-8-216-38127-3
ePDF: 979-8-216-38129-7
eBook: 979-8-216-38128-0

Typeset by Integra Software Services Pvt. Ltd.
Printed and bound in the United States of America

For product safety related questions contact productsafety@bloomsbury.com.

"In this rich and thought-provoking book, James William Coleman traces the origins of Tara from the primal 'enchanted garden' of our earliest ancestors to her role as an enlightened female Buddha and symbol of awakened wisdom and compassion. *Searching for Tara* weaves together history, myth, Western psychology and Buddhist teaching, illuminating the enduring power of the sacred feminine and its vital relevance for today's troubled world. Tara's roots may be deep and ancient, but through Coleman's clear devotion and the practical meditations offered in this book, Tara becomes accessible as a living presence for modern readers. Few books unite rigorous scholarship and authentic spiritual devotion so beautifully."

— ANNA HOWARD, author of *Quest for the Enlightened Feminine: Faith, Tara, and the Path of Compassion*

"I have been working in the field of mental health and recovery for over 35 years, and we know that awakening experiences enhance wellness and recovery from psychiatric illnesses, including addiction, in many ways. The meditation practices outlined in Coleman's clear and engaging book offer a compelling and effective adjunct for healing and transformation. A must read."

— MICHAEL MCGEE MD, Distinguished Life Fellow, American Psychiatric Association, author of *The Joy of Recovery*

"This book is an invaluable aid in understanding the feminine principle in Buddhist psychology and meditation practice. Readers will find new depths of appreciation for the Tara practices of ancient India and how their feminine side can be encountered and explored in meditation."

— JASON SIFF, Buddhist teacher and author of *Unlearning Meditation: What to Do When the Instructions Get in the Way*

"In this inspiring and engaging book, Buddha Tara is brought forth as a balm for our human condition and the intense challenges of life in our modern world. James Coleman is perfectly placed as a committed scholar and practitioner to share Tara with us. The book begins with his own deep experience of Tara initiated by personal challenges. A vast range of fascinating territory is then covered from archeology, mythology, psychology, gender issues, and the history of goddess cultures, but we end in a practical place of application and how to personally connect with the profound power of Buddha Tara. Excellent!"

— ROSE TAYLOR GOLDFIELD, Co-Founder of the Wisdom Sun Buddhist Community, author of *Training the Wisdom Body*

"Not only is this book a tour de force of clear and vivid analysis and intellectual originality, it's a joy to read. This is Coleman's most personal and direct articulation of a lifetime of scholarship, reflection, meditation, and intellectual devotion. He places Tara within the contexts of developmental psychology and the evolution of human consciousness. And by doing so, he establishes her unique world historical significance as, perhaps, our best contemporary example of unfettered Shakti energy—a Goddess turned Bodhisattva. Tara has blessed these pages with her beauty and grace. If you are only going to read one book on Tara or you are searching for the best single introduction to her unique Buddhaverse, this is the book for you."

— ROBERT INCHAUSTI PhD, author of *Thomas Merton's American Prophecy and Spitwad Sutras: Classroom Teaching as Sublime Vocation*

To Claudia, Larry, and Arnie for their support and insight, and to all my teachers who have shared the priceless gems of their wisdom.

Contents

Figures

Foreword

By Lama Palden Drolma

Our world is in the midst of a profound crisis, and Tara offers us a way forward to bring the masculine and feminine energies of our culture into harmony and balance. I am constantly amazed by the deep hunger for the wisdom of the divine feminine that I see all around us and how deeply Tara resonates, even with those who have no real background in Buddhism or spiritual practice.

We don't really have a complete archetype of the awakened feminine here in the West—a figure like Tara who embodies both wisdom and sexuality, nurturing love and fierce wrathful power. I have always felt a deep connection with Mary, the mother of Jesus. Yet she is seen only as the pure Madonna, and never allowed to be sexual or to display her fierceness. She even had to conceive Jesus non-sexually because sex was often seen as gross and sinful. But it is not just a matter of sexuality. The idea that spiritual women have not only wisdom, but a strong, wrathful inner power doesn't go over very well in the West either. This kind of split didn't exist in the pre-Christian goddess traditions of the West, but as this book shows, at some point the full vision of the divine feminine was eclipsed by the patriarchy, and there is a deep longing to get it back.

In Hinduism, the feminine is seen as *shakti*, the primordial cosmic energy of creation, while Vajrayana Buddhism emphasizes the vast openness of the feminine. The feminine is seen as the womb of the divine mother that holds us all. Without space, without emptiness, nothing would be able to exist. Her emptiness holds all of us in divine love, nourishes us, gives us life, sustains us. This wisdom of emptiness in Buddhism is therefore personified as Tara, Prajnaparamita, and other awakened female beings. The awakened feminine is said to be the mother of all the buddhas, because it is the nonconceptual openness of the feminine that brings us to awakening. Indeed, wisdom is itself the essence of the divine feminine.

In her aspect as divine mother, Tara nurtures all life and gives birth to the awakened ones, but she also manifests a fierce wrathful power that cuts through our problems and obscurations, and most especially through our deep-rooted ignorance. She is like our Mother Earth who supplies us with everything we need, but can also manifest earthquakes, hurricanes, tidal waves, and tornados. The divine mother is a compassionate loving presence who's always available to us, but she may display a terrifying ferocity if that is what we need to wake up.

If you start a Tara practice, you will develop a profound appreciation for her and the way she works in our lives. You may have very powerful experiences in the beginning, but it's not usually an instantaneous process. It often takes time before we feel we have a real relationship with her. In our daily lives, developing a relationship with someone requires love and dedication, and meditating on Tara works in the same way. As you get to know Tara and receive her blessings, you come to see that she is a reflection of your own true nature, and that you can actually become Tara and embody peace, love, generosity, and all her other qualities. Tara mirrors back to us our own awakened nature.

On a personal level, this practice helps us recognize that we have all Tara's awakened qualities and the potential for all her awakened activities in ourselves. The practice is simply to allow her qualities to flourish within ourselves, so that whatever is needed in any given situation can spontaneously manifest out of us. If a situation calls for a pacifying influence, for calming people or bringing them together, then that kind of activity will spontaneously arise. If the situation needs some enriching, perhaps some kind of Dharma teaching or other education, or generosity in any form, it will come out of us. The same is true for attracting people together or for the more fierce energy where new boundaries have to be set or old patterns ended.

In Buddhist tantra, we sometimes meditate ourselves as male figures, sometimes as female figures, and sometimes as the union of the female and the male. All of us have female and male aspects within ourselves. It's said that in the subtle energy body, all of the *bindu*, our drops of vital energy, are the union of the female and male buddhas. We practice to purify, transform, and liberate the masculine and feminine within us, and ultimately to bring them into complete union. In fact, emptiness and form, heaven and earth, male and female—all seeming dualities must be brought into union to fully realize our true nature. All dualities are inseparable, and in their final essence they are all wisdom and compassion united.

So as you practice, it doesn't matter whether you're female or male in your body. It doesn't matter what your gender is or where you come from, the more you practice Tara, the more you will come to embody her enlightened qualities, and the more you become an emanation of Tara in this world of crisis and confusion--offering her peace, wisdom, and love to all who will accept them. What matters is that we do the practice that is right for us and for the world.

This book is the product of one such transformative encounter with Tara, and the author's struggle to make sense of something that didn't fit within the narrow horizons of the Western rationalism in which he grew up. Each of us follows our own path, and each of us sees Tara from our own perspective, but there is something universal here as well, and I invite you to dive into this fascinating account of Tara's history and the promise she holds for our troubled world, and see what speaks to you.

Prologue

Tara changed my life in ways I never could have imagined. As so often happens, the catalyst was a personal crisis. It came in October 2016, when I had cataract surgery on my right eye. I was told it was a simple procedure, but complications left me with a detached retina that took three more emergency surgeries to reattach, and I had to have two more surgeries after that before things finally stabilized. After the third surgery, my doctor put a gas bubble in my eye. He told me that for the next three weeks I had to keep my head face-down all night long and for at least eight hours during the day. I was confronted with the terrifying prospect that I might lose most or all the vision in my right eye and that there was another cataract growing in the left, so my fear kept me highly motivated to follow his instructions to the letter. It wasn't easy. I laid awake most nights because of the back pain that strange sleeping posture caused, but the hardest part was keeping my head down during the day.

I'd had a regular meditation practice for more than twenty years before the first surgery, and I was determined to "bring my obstacles to the path." So I found a way to sit in a cross-legged meditation posture with my forehead resting face down on my desk, and there I sat for eight hours a day. For the first few days, I was awash in fear and confusion. Eventually, I started going through my mental catalog of meditation practices looking for something that might help, and I remembered White Tara. I had done a variety of other visualization practices before, but I didn't know much about the details of her practice. All I remembered was that she was associated with health and longevity and that seemed to be exactly what I needed.

I had seen countless images of White Tara over the years, so I just reached out from the depths of my suffering, repeated her mantra, and fixed her in my mind. The visualization became increasingly clear and vivid as time went by, and I began to feel her presence there in front of me. Then something happened I can't really explain. All the barriers between us dissolved, and I connected with an indescribable love and an openness so vast and powerful that it seemed to pervade the entire universe. After that something shifted, and none of the things I feared seemed to matter the way they did before.

Of course, such overwhelming experiences inevitably fade with time, but the insights they reveal often linger on. Ever since then, Tara has been the focus of my daily meditation, and as my life stabilized, my relationship with her only deepened. As an academic and a writer, I have struggled again and again to understand her ineffable feminine presence and how she transformed my life. Yet even though Tara remains as mysterious as ever, the attempt to make sense of it all has led to countless discoveries and delights, and this book is a product of that quest.

1

A Future That Has Not Yet Dawned

The scientific revolution and the vast economic transformation that accompanied it have remade the world in a few dazzling centuries. New technologies and new productive forces poured forth a vast cornucopia of wealth undreamed of until now, cured dread diseases, conquered the skies and the seas, and linked the world together in a vast interconnected web.

All these wonders dazzle the eye, and there's no question that our wealth and power have exploded, but what of our wisdom? What of the spiritual myopia that seems to have afflicted us? What of the loneliness and anxiety that is the inevitable companion of our newfound individualism? The material abundance we wreaked such havoc to produce has failed to bring us the happiness or the security it promised, and year by year, we've become more alienated, fearful, and angry. We hardly seemed to have noticed as the wonders of the natural world were pushed aside for the plowed field, the highway, and the skyscraper; as the air and land were fouled with pollution; and as one species after another was driven to extinction. Looking out from the third decade of the twenty-first century, it appears that we are finally facing a crisis that can no longer be ignored as the climate changes that our reckless greed has wrought threaten our very survival, and our political and social institutions seem to be collapsing under the weight of their own corruption.

While the crisis is obvious to anyone who cares to look, the way forward is not. We are well-positioned to craft a technological response, but we seem at a loss to understand the underlying social, psychological, and most especially the spiritual forces that lie at the root of the problem. No social changes so sweeping could possibly have left us unchanged, yet we seem unaware of our progressive alienation from nature or the way our personal reality has changed to accommodate the ever-growing demands of the ego.

To see the way ahead, we need a new understanding of our past that places our psychological and spiritual evolution at the center of the human story, not at its periphery. As a goddess, a Buddha, and an archetype of feminine spirituality, Tara is a figure uniquely suited to point the way beyond our profound alienation from the natural world and what appears to be an oncoming crisis of the patriarchal ego. Although Tara has her origins in the traditions of Vajrayana Buddhism, the boundless enlightened wisdom she embodies transcends the limits of any tradition, ideology, or gender identification. She speaks just as loudly to anyone who listens—female, male, or nonbinary, Hindu, Christian, Pagan, Muslim, Taoist, Jew, or skeptical materialist. Yet to most Westerners, Tara remains a strange and rather remote figure. The deeper I probed, the more obvious it became that Tara seems so alien because of the alienation of Western culture itself and our estrangement from the natural world and the verdant symbolic life of the unconscious mind. Tara doesn't seem alien because she leads us away from ourselves, but because she shows us the direction to *a future that has not yet dawned.*

We can only understand Tara and what she means for our lives if we understand the spiritual crisis of our times and the vast sweep of historical forces that brought us here. Of course, we usually prefer to tell our history as a series of great dramas–wars, revolutions, the glory of vast empires and their spectacular collapses with their countless heroes and villains. Exploring the development of human spirituality with all its mysterious subtleties is a very different task than recounting the exploits of our ancestors, and it requires as much insight and intuition as scientific precision. But if we step back and blur our vision a bit, three movements in the evolution of our spirituality appear, and for our purposes at least, they provide the most fruitful ground for understanding.

All this certainly doesn't mean that the tools of critical scientific analysis we've honed to such a fine edge are of no use here. The archaeologists carefully exhuming, cataloging, and analyzing the shards of our past; the ethnographers immersing themselves in tribal cultures and reporting what they see; the historians pouring over the vast expanse of the written record; and the sociologists, anthropologists, and philosophers, who have tried to make sense of it can provide the keys to understanding the inner lives of our ancestors and what they mean for us today if we can weave them together into one great tapestry. Yet no matter how hard we try, a certain mystery and ambiguity remain. What follows is as much a myth as a statement of some kind of objective fact, and like all myths it should be judged by what it tells us about ourselves and our future, not its truth or falsity.

***

Our search for Tara begins in what the great sociologist Max Weber called the "enchanted garden" of spirits and unseen forces inhabited by our most ancient ancestors. The archaeological record tells us that for most of human history, we lived in small communal groups that moved from place to place in response to the ever-changing seasons and the availability of food and other resources. Such nomadic foragers usually built some kind of simple structures, but they spent most of their time out of doors in the natural world on which they were completely dependent for their survival. The trees, the plants, the animals, even the rocks and streams were alive and sentient, and their magical world abounded with unseen spirits and other powerful beings. The relationship between the humans and the natural world was so close that the line often blurred. Powerful spiritual beings could enter into the bodies of the humans, and humans on some occasions could even become such beings and access their extraordinary powers. Our primal ancestors had no priests, temples, or holy books, and they saw no real separation between the religious and the secular. Spiritual life was shared by the whole community in, for example, rites of hypnotic dancing, drumming, and singing which might go on for days at a time, and become a vehicle for entrance into the ecstatic states that open the door to the world of the spirits. The denizens of the enchanted garden didn't worship those powerful beings from afar. Rather our ancient ancestors sought to come directly into the presence of the spirits and if possible even merge with them and channel their magical power.

I searched all the shards of evidence I could find to see if any of those powerful spiritual beings resembled Tara, but the archaeological record offered only tantalizing hints; and since our distant ancestors left no written records, I just couldn't tell. Most of what we do know about these people comes from studies of the small bands of hunters and gatherers who survived into modern times, and when combined with the archaeological record, they give a rich picture of the general outlines of their lives and their spirituality, but their particular myths and stories are another matter. Tens of thousands of years of social evolution have erased them from view.

The next movement of our spiritual evolution came as powerful new gods arrived in the enchanted garden demanding worship and obedience. Some of the earliest convincing evidence of deity worship comes from the people who lived in small farming villages in Europe and the Near East that the archaeologist Marija Gimbutas dubbed the "goddess cultures." Their Great Goddess was the living embodiment of the power of the feminine in the natural world, and she held sway over every aspect of life—birth, growing food, building shelter, death, and even rebirth. Since the goddess cultures show no evidence of kingship, constant warfare, or the vast inequalities of more advanced farming societies, it seems likely that the Great Goddess they worshiped shared much more in common with the powerful beings of the enchanted garden then the distant and fearful gods who succeeded her, and it is here that we see Tara's roots as a goddess most clearly.

As those villages were absorbed into vast empires with advanced agriculture, their simple egalitarianism was replaced by the rule of kings and noble landlords, and the powerful beings of the enchanted garden were slowly displaced by new gods who, like kings, were distant, wrathful beings demanding obedience and respect. Religious practice was separated from everyday life and taken over by professional priests, and the religious attitudes of many people underwent a radical transformation. Instead of merging with the powerful beings of the natural world, they came to worship these new gods from afar, offering them reverence and sacrifice.

When the ancient Sumerians invented the first written language, the Great Goddess was still a force to be reckoned with, but by then she had been joined by a host of powerful male and female competitors. As time went on and the patriarchy of agricultural society grew ever stronger, the male gods took control and the goddesses were fragmented into more specialized roles. Where monotheism replaced older religious beliefs, the goddesses were entirely banished and replaced by the single male God, and the control of religious institutions was consolidated in the hands of men.

Since the beginnings of full-fledged human language, we have always understood our world and our culture through myths, stories, and shared rituals. But the next great transformation of human spirituality begins as a radical new kind of thinking enters the historical record around the middle of the first millennium BCE—an era the German philosopher Karl Jaspers called the "Axial Age." Of course, mythological thought continues on in countless ways today, but the axial breakthrough created a new mode of understanding at a far higher level of abstraction than ever before. Such great thinkers as Confucius, Plato, Mahavira, Socrates, Mencius, Aristotle, and Siddhartha Gautama developed increasingly sophisticated conceptual systems in the attempt to rationally understand and manipulate the world. The particulars of their philosophies varied, but for the first time there were philosophies—new ways of looking at the world based on critical thought and careful systematic analysis that challenged the very foundations of their social world.

Many see a fundamental opposition between the demands of reason and the demands of the spiritual life, but the historical record paints a far more complex picture. The rational systematic thought so central to the axial breakthrough gave birth to the first theologies and the use of far more sophisticated religious concepts which opened vast new vistas of religious thought. When turned inward, it spawned the first organized systems with step-by-step instructions for meditation and spiritual practice which offered a more stable path to spiritual realization than the ecstatic rites of tribal life. Yet at the same time this new mode of thought also chipped away at the myths, the stories, and the magic of the enchanted garden. The first attack came from hegemonic monotheism which strove to banish any mythologies but its own. But it was the incredible success of the scientific revolution in the period from about 1500 to 1700 CE and of the materialistic philosophy that claimed to be its basis, that led to a thoroughgoing disenchantment of the world that often left no place for an enlightened being like Tara.

Yet the magic potency of the feminine could never be entirely repressed, and it reemerged in countless forms, such as veneration of the Virgin Mary and perhaps most powerfully in the wild ferment of the tantric movement in medieval India, where Tara first took on her modern form. Some say she began as a Buddhist version of the great Hindu goddess Durga who herself was a form of goddess Devi, the supreme creator and destroyer of the world. Over time, however, Tara came to be considered a fully enlightened Buddha. While her followers still called on her for help with their personal problems as they might a goddess, she is never shown with a husband or children, and there are no stories of her fighting with other gods, taking a heroic journey into the underworld, or displaying any of the jealousy or vitriol so common among the gods. Since a Buddha is a pure manifestation of awakened wisdom, Tara never plays out any kind of personal drama at all. Many still revered her as a goddess, but the highest goal of her practice was not to worship her. It was to merge with the enlightened wisdom and love she embodies. In other words, she represents a kind of return to the spiritual path of our most ancient ancestors. Like them, the *tantrikas* sought to cultivate deep ecstatic states, and merge with powerful beings that at least appear to be outside themselves. But if it was a return to the past, it was a return at a far higher level. When properly applied tantric meditation practices allow a focused control of the primal energies of life in a way that ecstatic dancing and self-mortification cannot. Perhaps more importantly to merge with Tara or some other tantric *yidam* is not just to merge with the spirits of nature, but with infinite enlightened awareness full of boundless love for all beings.

As important as all this is, something still seemed to be missing. When I ran across the pioneering work of the great Jungian psychologist, Erich Neumann, I realized there is a vast psychological dimension to our growth that's been ignored by historians and anthropologists. Like other Jungians, Neumann based his understanding on the incredible wealth of human myths and symbols, but tellingly, he showed how the historical evolution of the structure of the psyche and the individual developmental path each of us traverse follow a parallel course. Our prehuman ancestors lived in a kind of undifferentiated oneness with their environment and so does each newborn child. As the first glimmers of conceptual thought emerge, so does the sense of self and with it the terrifying recognition of how weak and limited we are, and how dependent we are on what Neumann called the "Great Mother." For the infant, of course, the great mother is an actual biological person, but for ancient humanity it was the overwhelming power of nature often symbolized by the all-powerful goddesses among whom Tara is sometimes included. As the developmental process continues, the fledgling ego struggles to separate itself from the mother, just as primitive humanity struggled to subdue its natural environment and impose a human order.

In classic mythology, this emerging ego is symbolized by the great heroes who slaughter their foes and rule as kings, but it seems that the reign of the great masculine ego that conquers the instinctive power of the Goddess may be coming to an end. The heroic struggles of the ego have indeed created undreamed of wonders, but they have also left unprecedented havoc and destruction, and a yawning spiritual void in their wake, and we are left to ponder what comes next. Will we continue to tear ourselves and our planet apart until some apocalyptic climax threatens our very existence? Will we respond with a medley of minor reforms that allow us to avoid disaster while never really freeing ourselves from the mire of our confusion? Or does some higher level of spiritual development await us?

The psychic forces symbolized by the goddess and her primal connection to nature, instinct, and the emotions, seem diametrically opposed to the powers of the will, the ego, and the rational self-control often symbolized by the hero. Yet neither a return to the warm comfort of the goddess's womb nor an even more forceful repression of her seductive power offer a viable way forward. There is, however, another great symbol that incorporates the wisdom of the goddess *and* the wisdom of the hero into a higher level of understanding. The classic image of a male Buddha sitting in the cross-legged lotus posture comes close. He seems to rest in complete peace and equanimity, embodying a wisdom far beyond any possible conflict. Yet at the same time, he also appears withdrawn and aloof from the chaos of this world of suffering, and at least to me, it is hard to see how he could represent a path forward for the struggling masses of humanity. If, however, we look at one of the images of Tara or another female Buddha, we get a very different feeling. She shows that same kind of transcendental peace, but at the same time she appears intimately connected to the life of the world. In many renderings, she has a radiant, loving smile and a glowing warmth, while her right leg is extended forward so that she can leap to the aid of anyone who suffers. She is both passionately involved in the world, and rooted in a transcendental wisdom that brings her beyond any kind of egocentric attachments and concerns. Although Neumann seems to have known little of Buddhist philosophy, at the end of his sweeping study of the archetype of the Great Mother he came to recognize Tara as the great symbol of the highest development of feminine spirituality. Seen more broadly, she seems to be a harbinger of a new stage of psychic development for women and men alike, for she combines the primal connection to nature of the Great Mother and the heroic power of the ego into a new synthesis that holds them both, feminine and masculine, in the vast emptiness of the awakened mind.

All that may sound intriguing, but I admit it is frustratingly difficult to understand what terms like "transcendent realization" or "awakened mind" really mean. No matter how much we try to pin her down, Tara always seems to slip away. Yet even though we cannot really capture Tara with our rational calculations, *we can become her.* That is to say, we can bring her enlightened wisdom into our daily lives. There is a whole toolkit of refined meditation techniques that allow us to at least temporarily merge with the awakened wisdom she embodies, and Chapter 7 explores some of these time-tested practices for those who wish to actualize Tara's mysterious wisdom in the chaos of our modern world. To me it's the most important chapter in the book. So even if you skip over the rest, I hope you will consider what it has to offer.

2

The Enchanted Garden

The obvious place to begin our search for Tara is with our primal ancestors, but there are so many stories about them it is hard to separate fact from fantasy. Some envision a lost age of peace and plenty where the goddesses ruled, while others scoff and insist that our past was a brutal struggle for survival and that it was the men who always dominated the spiritual world. So what do we really know about the spiritual lives of the ancient peoples who had no historians and left no written records? It may seem that the answer is "very little." The evidence is certainly spotty and inconclusive, and to make matters worse, the anthropologists who analyze such things are notoriously contentious and have had bitter disagreements about how to interpret it all.[1] Still, if we put the various sources we have together and use a little imagination, we can still paint a vivid picture of that long-lost world.

The first place to turn is to the archaeologists who have carefully analyzed the physical remains early humans left behind—from their bones to the tools and refuse they produced. Evidence for permanent human settlements comes only toward the end of the archaeological record and the first evidence of farming comes even later. So despite the efforts of a few recent revisionists,[2] there's little doubt that for most of human history we were nomads living off the land and moving from place to place in response to changing seasons and the availability of food. The tools early humans left behind show us that they used only the simplest technology and they probably never owned more than they could carry with them. The archaeological record tells us far less about the way people thought and what they believed, but it does leave us with some fascinating hints.

There may be no written records from those times, but what we do have are the remains of humankind's first artistic creations. Most of the art of the earliest humans was lost long ago, but amazing paintings and wall carvings from the Paleolithic era have survived in a few scattered caves, as have some sculptures that were made from durable materials such as stone or bone, and they offer a tantalizing glimpse behind the veil the millennia have drawn across our history.[3] There is, however, a problem. Our earliest ancestors who lived the simple, nomadic lifestyle left little by way of durable art. Those cave paintings and carved figures come from what anthropologists call "complex hunters and gatherers," who came after the first foragers and lived only in areas with usually rich environments. The European hunters who lived at the end of the last ice age were such people. In that time and place, vast herds of migrating animals would pass through narrow valleys, creating ideal hunting conditions. People there no longer needed to move around as much (and sometimes not at all), techniques for drying meat created the possibility of far better long-term food storage, social life seemed to grow more complex, and new kinds of art and handicrafts flourished. So this ancient art provides a window into a social world that evolved beyond the earliest patterns of human life, but not so far that it is unreasonable to suppose that the same spiritual realities held true in both.

The oldest cave art we know of comes from the island of Sulawesi in Indonesia, but the paintings found in Europe are far more extensive, and these same groups of peoples left other important artifacts—particularly the small carved figures that archaeologists have found scattered wherever they encamped. Their cave paintings are primarily of the animals of the hunt upon which early humans depended for their survival. There are a few human figures who appear to be male hunters, but they are far outnumbered by the animals. One of the most amazing finds was made by three teenage brothers in southern France in the early twentieth century. The caves and passageways they discovered, now known as the Caves of Trois Frères, are full of art dating from around 13000 BCE, and they strike many who have explored them as a kind of Paleolithic cathedral. Imagine crawling through forty yards of dark, claustrophobic tunnels sometimes no higher than a foot, and emerging into a great cavern covered with figures of every sort of animal etched into its surface—mammoths, bison, wild horses, reindeer, wolverines, musk oxen, bear, owls, rabbits, fish, and even rhinos. At the far end, the most famous and enigmatic of these images hovers fifteen feet above the floor. Known as the Sorcerer of Trois-Frères, because according to one early interpretation it represents a shaman or a magician, it has the legs of a man, the body antelope or an elk, humanlike arms that end in what appear to be paws, and a vaguely defined head with what may be human eyes—the uroboric fusion of human and animal.

Was this actually an image of a shaman, a powerful spiritual being, or a hunter trying to hide himself from his prey? This mysterious image refuses to give up its secrets even though it seems to resonate with some long-forgotten ancestral memory. The great mythologist Joseph Campbell suggests that this was a place where the men sought to merge with the spirit of the animals to ensure the success of the hunt. What we don't see, however, is as important as what we do; for there are no representations that look like the remote and powerful gods of the agricultural peoples.

Not far away, another system of caves in southern France at Lascaux contains its own master works of Paleolithic art. Like Trois-Frères, most of the paintings depict the animals of the hunt, but another highly revealing image shows a bison that has been eviscerated by a spear and is pointing its horns at the prone figure of what appears to be man with the head of a bird and a prominent erection. Next to him lies a stick topped with the image of another bird—a symbol still used by contemporary shamans.

Another remarkable figure, this one carved from a mammoth tusk, was found in a remote cave in what is now Germany. Not only is it far older than the paintings at Lascaux and Trois-Frères, it is one of the few ancient figurines that seems to represent a male. This "lion man" is about a foot long and appears to be a human male with the head of a lion—one more symbol depicting the fusion of human and animal (see Figure 2.1). Over and over again, this ancient art shows us the overwhelming importance of the animals of the natural world to our human ancestors, and their deep spiritual connections that allowed the humans to merge with the spirits of the animals and perhaps with other powerful beings as well.

The small carved figures that have been recovered from the mouths of caves and from other places where people actually lived, are radically different from the wall art. Instead of animals, they usually depict human females with pendular breasts, swollen bellies, and a prominent vulva, perhaps indicating pregnancy or at least ample fertility. Various scholars have claimed that these enigmatic figures were everything from Paleolithic pornography to all powerful mother goddesses, but the truth is that we really don't know. What does seem clear, as Joseph Campbell suggests, is that these figures reflected the great awe in which early humans held the female power of reproduction. These figures appear to set off the female realm of the camp, family, and children, from the male realm of the hunt

Figure 2.1 *Loewenmensch, the lion man from the Stadel cave in the Hohlenstein, Lonetal. Credit: Dagmar Hollmann, Wikimedia Commons, CC BY-SA 4.0 License.*

and the magic of the caves. But were those figures representations of powerful and distant goddesses, of the spirits of the natural world, an ideal type of actual human women, erotica, or something else? It is unlikely that the women among these foraging groups actually looked like those images, so it doesn't seem they were a representation of actual people. Likewise, although those images certainly have an erotic charge, if that were their primary purpose, we would also expect to find statues of couples or males with erections, and we do not. On the other hand, those figurines do not have the crowns and symbolic embellishments we would expect for the figures of a god. Nor are there any of the depictions of deity worship which are so prominent in later art.

One possible exception is the ancient bas-relief of a naked woman carved into the wall of a rock shelter in Laussel in southern France (see Figure 2.2). She has the great hips, breasts, and belly typical of the art of that era. She is completely naked and has no crown or jewelry as a goddess might, but her right hand holds what must have been a powerful symbol. It appears to be a curved bison horn, but it brings to mind the crescent moon, and it is marked by thirteen lines which might represent the thirteen months of the lunar calendar and therefore be connected to the cycles of menstruation. There were certainly many goddesses from the pantheons of the agricultural societies who were associated with the powers of the moon, so this image may be one of the earliest known depictions of the Great Goddesses. However, since we know that many hunting and gathering societies have female as well as male shamans, and that some cave paintings clearly depict shamanic activity, it seems more likely that she represents a powerful female shaman calling on the powers of the moon to bring fertility and abundance, or perhaps she is one of the powerful beings that are so abundant in the primal worldscape of more recent hunters and gathers.

To flesh out the bare skeleton of facts from the archaeological record, we must turn to the studies of foragers who lived the nomadic life and survived into the modern era. Unfortunately, by the time ethnographers began their studies, modern technological society had spread to the farthest corners of the earth, leaving few cultures untouched. Still, if we look at these far-flung groups long enough, we can see some obvious similarities that don't appear to come from outside influences.

Figure 2.2 *Venus of Laussel from Marquey, France. Pre-historic statue from 18 to 20,000 years ago. Credit: Wikimedia Commons, CC BY 3.0 License.*

Imagine that you live in one of those nomadic societies. There are twenty or thirty people in your band, and you know everyone in the most intimate possible way. Although your little band moves around in response to changes in the seasons and animal life, it's always in the same area, and you know each mountain, stream, and river as well as you know your own family. Conflicts can easily erupt among people with such close daily contact (archaeological studies suggest that those in some groups of ancient foragers may have been more likely to fall victim to lethal violence than we are today), but there is so much you share that binds you all together—the common effort of the hunt, sharing food and resources, and communal singing and dancing that could go on for weeks at a time. Of course, some people in your band will be more respected than others, a great hunter or a wise old woman, for example, and perhaps there is someone who bullies others to try and run the show, but if the small nomadic societies that survived long enough for ethnographers to study are any indication, there are unlikely to have been any official chieftains, presidents, or kings. Important decisions are made by consensus, and anyone who tries to assume too much power and authority risks censure from the group.

The rhythm of your life comes from your intimate connection to the natural world. You wake up to the songs of birds and go to sleep to the chirping of insects. All day long you stay alert to the sights and sounds of the animals and plants around you to find food, avoid an unpleasant sting, or just because they're such an important part of your world. Unless you find shelter in one of the little huts you or your friends and family have built from sticks and leaves, you are never apart from the open spaces.

To some of us this may sound like an ideal way to live and to others pure savagery, but whatever you might think, it's clear that theirs was a radically different life from the one we know today. But does that mean that their spiritual concerns were so far removed from our own? It's clear that they didn't have any religion as we know it—no priests, churches, mosques, or temples, no systematic body of beliefs, and no holy books. Their rituals and beliefs were woven seamlessly into their everyday lives, and they recognized no separation between the religious and the secular. It was their relationship with nature that formed the core of their spirituality and the core of their lives. Their whole world was alive and aware—not just the humans and other animals, but the plants, the rivers and streams, even the sky and the earth. They also shared their world with non-human people—spirits and powerful beings—who, though they are usually concealed from the humans' everyday perception, were very much a living reality. The great German sociologist Max Weber put it aptly when he said that our ancestors lived in an "enchanted garden" full of wonder and mystery.

The relationship between the humans and the natural world was often so close that the line blurred. Humans became animals. Animals became human. Powerful spiritual beings entered into the bodies of humans, and humans could on some occasions become such beings and access their extraordinary powers. Numerous ethnographers have remarked on the kind of reverence and awe these people felt for it all. The incredible beauty of the waterfall, the fierce power of the jaguar, the stillness of the night were all a part of the sacred landscape of their lives and their psyches—a landscape deeply rooted in the unique features of the particular place in which they lived.

Huston Smith, the historian of religion, tells a story about Oren Lyons, the first member of the Onondaga tribe of the Iroquois to attend college. When he returned to his reservation for his first break from college, his uncle invited him on a fishing trip. Perhaps sensing Oren was a little taken with himself, his uncle waited until they were in the middle of the lake and then asked, "Oren, you must be pretty smart after all they are teaching you in college, so let me ask you a question. Who are you?" Oren tried to give the usual answers to such a question: I'm your nephew. A man. An Onondagan. A human being. But his uncle batted down each one, until Oren was reduced to silence. Finally, he asked his uncle to tell him who he is. And his uncle replied, "Do you see that bluff over there? Oren you *are* that bluff. And that giant pine on the other shore? Oren, you *are* that pine. And this water that supports our boat? You *are* this water."[4]

A similar story comes from the anthropologist Colin Turnbull, who spent years living among the Mbuti pygmies in what was then the Belgian Congo. Turnbull often heard them talk about something called the *molimo* as an "animal of the jungle." But as the pygmies came to accept him and began to open up, he found that it was actually the name of a kind of musical instrument as well as a ritual that pygmy men performed at times of crisis in which that instrument played a central role. When one member of the tribe died unexpectedly, Turnbull was finally invited to join in the ritual. Every night for two months, someone would sing into a long pipe and use it to make strange sounds that mimicked the animals of the forest, while the other men would sing and dance and answer its call. The women, on the other hand, would all stay in their huts and pretend to believe that the sound came from some animal of the forest and not from their menfolk. Turnbull found the whole thing puzzling and finally prevailed upon an elder to explain. While whittling away at a new bow he was making, wise old Moke told him, "The forest is a father and mother to us" and "gives us everything we need." The forest is good to us, so when things go wrong "it must be because the forest is sleeping, and not looking after its children. So what do we do? We wake it up. We wake it up by singing to it, and we do this because we want it to awaken happy. Then everything will be well and good again." Once it has awakened, "we sing to the forest, because we want it to share our happiness."[5] The forest is of overwhelming importance to the pygmies, and to them it is every bit as alive and sentient as they are. Indeed, during the *molimo* the distinction between the forest and its humans seems to disappear.

Since the *molimo* ritual was performed almost exclusively by men, it might appear to reflect some kind of patriarchal system among these foragers, but Turnbull soon discovered that there was far more gender balance than it might appear. One night he saw an old woman, who was visiting from another band, take over the *molimo* ritual and relegate the men to a secondary role. While the other women came out and surrounded the ritual fire singing *molimo* songs that only men were supposed to know, this old woman danced around and around until, to Turnbull's amazement, she literally danced into one side of the fire and out the other. All these events must have seemed quite unremarkable to the Mbuti, for the next morning they went back to their daily routines without a word of discussion.

The !Kung people who live on the western edge of the Kalahari Desert in Southern Africa, follow a similar pattern. The "trance dances" that allow participants to enter a state of altered consciousness (*!kia)* are a central religious rite, but there is little or no gender inequality—some dances are led by women and others by men. Such gender balance is not, however, universal in nomadic foraging bands. Among the Aboriginals of Australia, such as the Mardudjara studied by Robert Tonkinson,[6] the men often monopolize the important ritual activities, keeping many of them secret from the women and threatening any woman who finds them out.

Festive rituals of singing and dancing are common to people in small-scale societies from around the world, and if you look through the lens of our Western culture it may seem they are worshiping some kind of primitive gods. But the idea that there is a distant all-powerful god or gods who demand worship and sacrifice is entirely alien to them. If those ceremonies have any purpose beyond sheer enjoyment, it is to seek union with the powerful beings they invoke—not to worship them. When a Native American does a buffalo dance, he is not worshiping buffalos. He is becoming a buffalo and thereby gaining the power for a successful hunt.

Ellen Basso, who studied the Kalapalo people who live in an extremely isolated area of Brazil, tells us that sound is vitally important to them, and that they classify everything by the sound it makes. The powerful beings who were "there at the beginning" express themselves through music. Human beings express themselves through speech, while animals have calls, and inanimate objects just make noises. The Kalapalo celebrate great festivals dedicated to the powerful beings that can take months to organize and rehearse, and involve elaborate body painting, flower decoration, masks, and especially music accompanied by a kind of shuffling body movement. As Basso puts it, "Musical performance is associated with powerful beings and is a means to communicate with them …." But the communication does not occur

> by singing *to* a powerful being but by singing them *into being*. Highly focused mental images of the powerful being are created

> in the minds of the performers by means of the performance .... There is a consequent merging of the self with what is sung about; just as in myth powerful beings participate in human speech, so in ritual humans participate in *itseke* (powerful beings) musicality and thereby temporarily achieve some of their transformative power.[7]

Brian Hayden gives this account of a ritual that took place on the other side of the world in the Australian desert that transformed a man into a powerful being. While a group of men beat out entrancing rhythms and droned nasal chants for hours on end, a man

> opened a vein in his arm, letting the blood pour out, enough to fill a small bowl. Then, with the help of others he decorated his body with white and red plant fluff, using his blood to make it stick to his body in strange ritual shapes, shapes completely unknown in the natural world. Gradually, the transformation took place until at last it was complete. The man was no longer merely human but has been totally transformed into his totemic ancestor in every movement, look and feeling.[8]

The Australian aboriginals lived in relative isolation for over 50,000 years until their land was invaded by seagoing Polynesians and later by European colonialists. Australia is the only continent that never experienced what is called the "neolithic revolution"—the development of farming and more advanced stone tools—so some argue that the aboriginals are therefore closer to our ancient ancestors than any other surviving peoples. But no cultures are static for such vast lengths of time, and if their technology was simpler, in many ways their spiritual life was more complex. Most tribal people believe in some kind of spirit world, but for the aboriginals "the Dreaming," as they call it, is of overwhelming importance.

Their everyday world is much like ours, but behind that world is the timeless "everwhen" of the Dreaming, from which everything comes and to which everything returns. The Dreaming is the home of the "ancestral beings" who from our Western standpoint appear to be the creators of the world. But as sociologist Robert Bellah puts it, "[T]here is no idea of a beginning before creation, or even of creation. The forming activity of the ancestral beings is as much present as past."[9] While most people in tribal cultures only seek union with the powerful being in ritual and dance, the aboriginals devote their entire lives to it. Huston Smith writes:

> We are inclined to say that when the Arunta [an aboriginal people] go hunting, they mime the exploits of the first archetypal hunter, but this distinguishes them from the archetype too sharply. It is better to say that they enter the mold of their archetype so completely that each *becomes* the First Hunter; no distinction remains. Similarly for other activities, from basket weaving to lovemaking. Only while they are conforming their actions to the model of some archetypal hero do the Arunta feel that they are truly alive, for in those roles they are immortal.[10]

Almost everyone in these primal cultures seems to share in dances, songs, and rituals that bond them together and bring them into the presence of the powerful beings. Entry into the world of spirits may also occur spontaneously, for example, from a revelatory dream in which a powerful being appears to the sleeper or as part of a miraculous recovery from a deadly illness. More than mere contact with the powerful beings such revelations sometimes involved world-shattering ecstatic trances that lead beyond the states of everyday consciousness. Take, for example, the !Kung San people of the Kalahari Desert. As with so many indigenous peoples, their traditional way of life of has largely been lost. When anthropologist Richard Lee studied them in the early 1960s, however, what might be called community "trance dances" still played an important part in their spiritual life and enabled successful dancers to enter an ecstatic state that brought them into the presence of the powerful beings and often gave them the power to heal the sick. Westerners often imagine tribal dances like these as nothing more than a festive party, but becoming a healer is a long and difficult path requiring determination and the capacity to withstand intense physical pain, as well as the guidance of a mentor and other experienced practitioners. Nonetheless, most of the young !Kung that Lee encountered wanted to become healers, and many of them did. Lee estimated that half the adult men and a third of the women had achieved *!kia*—the trance state that allows entry into the spirit world—a far greater percentage of the population than ever reach equivalent states through meditation or psychoactive drugs in today's society.

The !Kung believe they have a substance in the pit of their stomach called *n/um* that heats up when they do their ritual dances. After hours of dancing, it boils, rises up the spinal cord, and explodes into the brain—an extremely painful process especially for a novice. Many are afraid they will lose control or even die, and leave the dance before they reach *!kia*. Teachers often go into trance with their students to help them along the way—massaging them and rubbing sweat into various parts of their bodies. As their *n/um* builds up, enormous energy courses through the dancer's body. Their legs tremble, their chest heaves, their throat goes dry, and strange visions flood their senses. When they first enter *!kia*, the inexperienced may collapse on the ground where they are massaged and supported by the other dancers, or they may go crazy and run off into the bush or perhaps even straight into the campfire, but with the help of the elders most eventually learn to control the power of the *n/um* and grow more comfortable with the *!kia* state. Once someone has mastered *!kia*, they may go on to become a healer with the ability to drive off the spirits of the dead, who are the cause of most sickness. As one healer put it, "When we are *!kia* we always change into something else. We can see things that ordinary people can't ... Your mind goes blank. You don't feel any pain. The ground seems to be spinning. We are different, a little bit like a ghost ourselves. And if the dead are there, we can see them."[11] Once they are in *!kia*, the healer either by herself or in groups cajoles, pleads, argues, and if necessary does battle with the spirits of the dead to make them leave the living in peace.

Entry into such ecstatic states may occur in solicitude as well. In some Native American cultures, the young men are expected to undertake a "vision quest" as part of their transition to adulthood. Although it may not transform them all into healers, it does bring them into ecstatic contact with the powerful beings. The quest usually begins with a series of rituals led by the elders after which the initiate goes off on a solitary retreat to a holy place, fasts, prays, and cries out until a vision of some powerful being, often in animal form, comes to him. In this momentous event, the initiate creates what is often a lifelong bond with that powerful being who helps guide and support him.

Initiation rituals like these often require endurance and the willingness to suffer for the sake of the group. Among the complex hunters and gatherers of the Northwest coast, for example, initiates were often dragged from their home to special ceremonial locations where they were subject to all kinds of physical and mental assaults. "For four days, with constant drumming and singing, initiates were blindfolded, stripped, forbidden to talk or move, deprived of sleep, dehydrated, placed under heavy covers, starved, teased, grabbed, lifted, bitten, hit, and punched in order to make them 'die.'"[12] Some of them had to run barefoot in the snow until they fell exhausted, swim in ice-cold water carrying heavy stones, or pierce or cut their own skin.

Another common path to transcendence is the use of specially prepared psychoactive drugs. Napoleon Chagnon writes that among the Yanomano,[13] a group who practiced simple farming in the Amazon rainforest:

> Contact with the hekura (powerful beings) is achieved by taking drugs. Particularly adept shabori (shaman) can contact their hekura with only a pinch of drug, which they inhale directly from their fingers. Most of them, however, take a large dose of the drug by means of the hollow blowing tube. [The drug is placed at the end of a long tube and forcefully blown into their nose by another tribesman.] The shabori then prances back and forth in front of his house and chants to the demons [powerful beings] he attempts to control, enjoining them to descend on enemies and cause them sickness. If he is curing someone, he chants before the house of the patient, rubs him, massages him, and draws the evil spirit causing the sickness to some extremity, such as an arm or leg. Then he sucks or pulls the spirit out and carries it away from the sick person, either vomiting it out or throwing it away, depending on how he extracted it originally.[14]

All these paths to the spiritual realm may seem to have little in common, but they follow a similar pattern. Whether by endless dancing and chanting, fasting, pain, extreme temperatures, partial asphyxiation, loss of blood, or mind-altering drugs, the seekers are pushed beyond the normal limits of their minds, and the habits of perception and thought that govern mundane reality collapse. Once this occurs, there is a radical alteration of consciousness. Numinous energy flows through their body, and they enter into the mysteries of the spirit world.

In some cultures, like the !Kung, ecstatic entrance into the spirit world is a common experience. In others, it is confined to religious virtuosos who gain prestige and status from their spiritual feats. Such people are sometimes referred to as "shaman"—a word that originally came from the Evenki language and was used in Russian to describe the healers among the native peoples of Siberia. The word is much more broadly used today and includes anyone from indigenous cultures who gains special powers from their connection to the spirit world and even a few people from the rich industrialized nations. In indigenous cultures the central role of a shaman is almost always that of healer, but in some cultures they are also sorcerers, and if they are, they are likely to hold a very different relationship to their peers. If they are good at their craft, shamanic healers are highly respected, but if they also perform sorcery or are believed to do so, they are likely to be feared as well, and that combination of respect and fear places them at a distance from their fellows. Moreover, the social consequences of those two roles are radically different. Ethnographers have taken numerous pictures of shamanic healing rituals that show a shaman surrounded by the friends and family of the patient supporting and encouraging the shaman's efforts to drive off the evil spirits that are causing the illness. It is clearly a community effort that binds people together. Yet if that illness is believed to be caused by the curse of another shaman or sorcerer, things are radically different. Instead of bringing people together, it can set off a struggle of neighbor against neighbor as they seek to find who is to blame, just as we saw during the famous "witch hunts" in the European cultures. If the shaman can identify the culprit, they may be called upon to curse them in return or vigilante justice may ensue.

Everyday life in the enchanted garden was grounded by a visceral connection to the natural world that, I think, is difficult for us moderns to understand. And that profound connection to nature is the soil in which all primal spirituality is rooted. The powerful spirits that populated their world were not just archetypal symbols, but a vital, living presence. No matter how much I searched, though, I could not be sure if an early analog of Tara was to be found among the powerful beings. What did leap out with striking clarity was how similar the spiritual practices among the hunters and gatherers that survived into modern times were to the tantric practices I knew from Tibetan Buddhism. Anyone who has ever done the Buddhist practice of *tummo* or the Hindu practice of *kundalini*, for example, is bound to be struck by their similarities to the trance dances of groups like the !Kung. Those primal rituals may be more wild and uncontrolled, but the idea that you build up a fiery energy in the belly which then rises up to the head in an ecstatic explosion follows exactly the pattern as those more sophisticated tantric practices. Even more striking are the similarities in the relationship primal peoples have with the powerful beings, and the relationship tantric practitioners have to their *yidam* (the enlightened being who is the object of their meditation). The ultimate goal of Tara practice is not to venerate her as you might a god, but to merge with her, and in some sense to actually become her; just as someone from a primal culture might become "first hunter" or a Kalapalo *itseke*. As we will see, there are profound differences between a Buddha like Tara and the spiritual beings of our primal ancestors, but there is no denying the common ground on which their practices rest or their roots in the mysterious splendor of the enchanted garden.

Sources

Unlike today, the study of religion was a central concern of many of the great classical sociologists. Although his work relied on the often inadequate sources that were available to him in the late nineteenth and early twentieth centuries, the brilliance of Max Weber's theoretical approach to the sociology of religion is beyond question.

His exploration of religious themes runs throughout his work, but his *Sociology of Religion* (trans. Ephraim Fischoff, Boston: Beacon Press, 1963) is the most relevant to this chapter. Although his orientation is more explicitly Durkheimian, the contemporary sociologist Robert Bellah's encyclopedic *Religion in Human Evolution: From the Paleolithic to the Axial Age* (Cambridge, MA: Belknap/Harvard, 2011) provided a wealth of useful information. While Huston Smith's classic work *The World's Religions: Our Great Wisdom Traditions* (HarperSanFranciso, 1993) is much shorter, it is full of elegant insights that I found extremely useful.

The ancient cave paintings and sculptures examined in this chapter are well-known to the public, and they have been the subject of countless theories and interpretations. I found those of the American mythologist Joseph Campbell most convincing. See his *Primitive Mythology: The Masks of God, Volume 1* (Novato, CA: New World Library, 2021; originally published 1959). I have long been fascinated by the ethnographies of the hunters and gatherers and horticulturalists who survived into modern times, and they were an invaluable resource for this chapter. My favorite is Colin Turnbull's classic on the BaMbuti pygmies, *The Forest People* (New York: Touchstone, 1961). Richard Lee's work *The Dobe !Kung* (New York: Holt Rinehart & Winston, 1984) is more academically written, but just as valuable. Other useful works include Robert Tonkinson, *The Mardudjara Aborigines, Living the Dream in Australia's Desert* (New York: Holt Rinehart & Winston, 1978), Robert Knox Dentan, *The Semai: A Nonviolent People of Malaya* (New York: Holt Rinehart & Winston, 1979), Napoleon Chagnon, *Yanomano: The Fierce People* (New York: Holt, Rinehart and Winston, 1968), Ellen Basso, *A Musical View of the Universe: Kalapalo Myth and, Ritual Performances* (Philadelphia: University of Pennsylvania Press, 1985), and Raymond Firth, *We the Tilopia: A Sociological Study of Kinship in Primitive Polynesia* (New York: American Book

Company, 1936). For a cautionary tale of the way the pressures of the contemporary world can transform a traditional people who still remain on the land, see Allyn Maclean Stearman, *Yuqui: Forest Nomads in a Changing World* (New York: Holt Rinehart & Winston, 1989). A good general summary of what we know about the foraging peoples is Carol R. Ember's "Hunter-Gatherers" in C. R. Ember, ed. *Explaining Human Culture.* Human Relations Area Files, https://hraf.yale.edu/ehc/summaries/hunter-gatherers, 2020. Brian Hayden's *Shamans Sorcerers and Saints* (Washington, DC: Smithsonian Institution, 2003) provides an insightful exploration of the various techniques traditional people used for entering ecstatic states. The single most influential work on "Shamanism" is Mircea Eliade's *Shamanism: Archaic Techniques of Ecstasy* (Princeton: Princeton University Press, 1964, originally published 1951). Eliade made a specific list of the essential characteristics of shamanism which some later scholars have criticized as narrow and inaccurate. Manvir Singh's recent book *Shamanism: The Timeless Religion* (New York: Knopf, 2025) takes the opposite approach using such a broad definition that in addition to traditional spirit healers everyone from Jesus and the hebraic prophets, to Joseph Smith and most contemporary Pentecostalists would be considered shaman. Moreover, while Eliade saw a monotheism not so unlike his own Roman Catholicism at the core of shamanistic spirituality, Singh sees shamanism primarily as offering a "simulated reality" aimed at meeting the psychological needs of its participants.

3

The Coming of the Gods

Those small female figurines and a few of the wall carvings we discussed in the last chapter are about all I could find when I scoured the meager archaeological record looking for Tara's roots in the Paleolithic Era. If we move forward to the time when people first began farming to supplement the diet they got from fishing, hunting, and gathering wild foods, things are different. As people settled down in more-or-less permanent villages, their production of paintings, pottery, and durable artifacts exploded. Although millennia went by before they created complex written languages, the walls of the buildings they constructed, their pottery, and the figurines they created were often covered with symbols, and even the shapes of the objects they produced were rich with religious meaning. Such symbols are, of course, harder to interpret than written scripts, but they can speak to us in a language of their own if we listen. I hear a story of a remarkable epoch before the brutal hierarchies of the agricultural states took control, when human culture reached a high level of sophistication and the power of the Great Goddess from whom Tara later emerged was on full view.

The Great Goddess

A kind of slow-motion social revolution started around 10,000 years ago, when humans first began to farm and use domestic animals for food and milk. At the onset, farming was a fairly simple, small-scale affair intended only to supplement the food from foraging activities. Over time it allowed more and more people to live in permanent villages, and transformed virtually all aspects of human life including our spirituality.

At first, the development of farming may have led to a significant increase in the economic and political power of women, as the food derived from male hunting activities became less important and simple forms of farming, carried on primarily by women, became the staple source of food. As this process unfolded, women gained prestige and power rivaling that of men.

An example from among the societies that survived long enough for ethnographers to study are the Iroquois people of what is now the Northeastern United States. In traditional Iroquois society, women grew and prepared most of the food, husbands lived with their wife's family, property passed through the mother's lineage, each longhouse had its own council of women, and an assembly of the clan mothers selected the chief (who was male) and they could remove him if they deemed him unworthy. This is not to say that the traditional Iroquois were some kind of a matriarchy. They were a warlike people who raided their neighbors and often tortured captives to death or kept them as slaves. Since the men were the warriors, they had their own sphere of power. And even the most traditional Iroquois lived in a very different environment from the people of the earliest farming societies. The archaeological evidence from those societies does not usually show the telltale signs of the constant warfare that was so central to Iroquois life, probably because there was enough good farmland to go around and, therefore, less need to defend it with violent force.

The archaeological record of Europe and the Middle East has been more carefully studied than anywhere else, and it is there we find the best evidence of what some of the early farming societies were like. More than any other, it is the great archaeologist Marija Gimbutas who has been responsible for bringing to light the ancient cultures that practiced simple farming in what she called Old Europe (southeastern Europe and Anatolia) some 4,000 years before the first great agricultural civilizations emerged in the Fertile Crescent.

Unlike the warlike pastoralists whose repeated invasions may ultimately have destroyed these cultures, archaeological evidence suggests that the people of these Goddess-worshiping cultures were far more peaceful and egalitarian. Archaeologists have found no military fortifications, no images of war gods, no depictions of battles or great warriors, no kingly burial sites, and no great palaces. What they have found are modest shrines full of images of the Goddess, but interestingly, those shrines were often combined with workshops for making pottery, weaving cloth, and baking bread—things women did that apparently were considered sacred activities.

Archaeologists have also found the remains of a huge array of figurines from these cultures which Gimbutas estimates to number well over 100,000. The vast majority of them are female, so their makers appear to be the spiritual descendants of the artists of the Paleolithic era who left us those small female statues. These creations must have fulfilled some kind of religious purpose, but were they actually goddesses? That is to say, were they merely seen as fellow denizens of the enchanted garden of spirits and powerful beings, or did these early farming societies actually worship the beings those figurines represented? Since the remains of the shrines we mentioned not only contained altars and female statues and images, but a variety of ritual instruments and even some evidence of animal sacrifice, it appears that they were indeed worshiping a goddess. As humans moved away from their natural environment into village settlements, it seems they felt an increasing need to demonstrate their reverence for nature in her form as the Great Goddess.

Because these peoples left no written language we can decipher, we don't know their myths or stories. It seems likely that the host of female figurines and images they left behind depicted different forms of a single great deity, but if we were able to uncover their myths we might find that they were actually worshiping numerous separate goddesses. Before we examine the different forms the Great Goddess took in these ancient cultures, perhaps we should listen to what Gimbutas has to tell us about her overall meaning:

> The Goddess in all her manifestations was the symbol of the unity of all life in Nature. Her power was in water and stone, in tomb and cave, in animals and birds, snakes and fish, hills, trees, and flowers.[1] [The] sophisticated, complex art surrounding the Neolithic goddess is a shifting kaleidoscope of meaning: she personified every phase of life, death, and regeneration. She was the Creator from whom all life—human, plant, and animal—arose, and to whom everything returned.[2]

The Goddess was the source from which we all came. She was the force that brought the bounty of the harvests and sustained our lives. She was bringer of death, and in its time, she also brought rebirth and regeneration. She was the embodiment of the miraculous cyclical power of the natural world. To worship her was to liberate ourselves from the sense of separation and commune with all existence.

The most obvious representations of her life-giving power are the ubiquitous figurines of a pregnant goddess that are found throughout Europe and the Near East. She is depicted with an extended belly, either sitting or semi-reclining with her knees bent and legs raised in the birth-giving position, and often with a swollen vulva. Birthing was apparently a sacred act, and the remains of birthing rooms, or perhaps more accurately birthing shrines, have been found that were colored red, the color of blood and of life, and decorated with stylized figures on the walls representing women giving birth. The Pregnant Goddess did more than just give human life, she sustained it as well, and her images have often been found in areas associated with ovens and bread baking. One of the most famous is an eight thousand-year-old statue found in the ruins of a grain bin in Çatalhöyük, an ancient town in what is now southern Turkey (see Figure 3.1). In this amazing work of art, the Goddess is seated on a lion throne (felines symbolize female deities and their power in many of the world's mythological systems), and her regal bearing gives testimony to her divine power as her swollen breasts and belly do to her ability to give life.

In her role as life-sustainer, the Goddess often appears commingled with various animals that abound in nature. The snake, with its phallic symbolism, is often her companion, sometimes coiled around her or

Figure 3.1 *Seated Goddess from Çatalhöyük, Turkey. Neolithic age (about 6000-5500 BCE). Credit: Roweromaniak, Wikimedia Commons, CC BY-SA 2.5 License.*

to one side, and she herself sometimes appears as a Snake Goddess. In these images, she is sitting yogi-like or squatting with snake-shaped limbs and sometimes a snakelike head. As the Fish Goddess, she has the body of a fish with a human face, breasts, and vulva. The fish represents the watery world from which comes the life-giving power of the womb, but the most common animal form of the Goddess was probably the bird—an animal that soars through the transcendent heavenly skies, then returns to rest in this terrestrial world and sometimes even dives into the watery depths. As the Bird Goddess, she often has a face with a beak-like nose, atop a long, slender neck and a human body. Sometimes her body is decidedly egg-shaped which reminds us not only of her life-giving power, but also the fact that in many mythologies the world life originally came from a great cosmic egg.

The Goddess also appears in a bird-like form in her role as the bringer of death, and in this case, she is a raptor. Many of these goddess-worshiping peoples practiced excarnation—that is, they did not bury their dead, but left them in a special place where birds would strip away their flesh. The bones that remained would later be interred in a shrine. So, it is not surprising that the Goddess of Death appears as a vulture with human feet and sometimes a human vulva. The owl—that mysterious bird of the night with a humanlike face and enormous round eyes—was another of her forms.

Archaeologists commonly find figurines of what Gimbutas called the "stiff white goddess" in the places where human remains were interred. She has a slender body and, sometimes, owl-like eyes. Her breasts are unusually small, for her role here is not that of nurturer, but she typically has a prominent vulva—a powerful symbol not of death but of female power and regeneration. Death was seen as a return to the great maternal womb, which was also the source of rebirth and restoration. In many later mythologies like those of the

Greeks and Romans, the land of the dead was a dark and fearful place from which there was no return, but in the goddess cultures death was simply part of the cycles of nature, and rebirth was bound to follow death, just as so many plants die in the winter, return to the soil, and are reborn in the spring.

In advanced agricultural societies, the power of the gods and the power of the kings were intimately related. Indeed, many sociologists feel that the relationship between a person and her god was modeled on the relation of peasants to their lords. Since the goddess cultures apparently had no kings, it follows that the Great Goddess they worshiped would have been more like the powerful beings of the enchanted garden than the terrifying gods of agricultural societies. If this intuition is right, then it is in this enchanted garden that we see Tara's origins most clearly, not as a frightening and arbitrary ruler, but as a manifestation of the fiery feminine energy that makes life possible in this world.

Gods and Kings

If you were to examine one of the cuneiform tablets from ancient Sumer, it wouldn't look like anything special. Just baked pieces of clay full of little triangular markings. None of the exotic hieroglyphs of the Egyptians or the elegance of Chinese calligraphy. But they nonetheless mark a turning point in human history—our first complete written language. Those ancient tablets open a door into the world of our ancestors that figurines, paintings, and contemporary ethnographies cannot. The archaeological record gives only hints about the myths and stories ancient people told, but reading those myths from the ancient texts brings them to life before our eyes. There is, however, a problem. Writing first came into use in large-scale agricultural societies, and if we look at the broad sweep of human history, we see that they were among the most unequal and patriarchal of any our species has known. Only an educated few could read or write, and the scribes who first set down those ancient myths were invariably part of the religious elite or at least served its purposes. When we read the story of one god conquering another or a god punishing the people for some kind of offense, they are as likely to be a reflection of the changing political and religious balance of power in those ancient societies as an accurate reflection of the beliefs of most people. The myths of the common people, on the other hand, were seldom set down in writing. We can be sure that everyone knew of the gods of the state religion and their demands, but it is far less clear what average people believed or the gods and goddesses they turned to in times of trouble.

What is clear is that the entry of a vast pantheon of new gods into the enchanted garden marked a startling religious transformation. As we have seen, the world of nomadic foragers was a magical place full of countless spirits and unseen forces. They sometimes told stories about distant and powerful beings who created the world and its people. But such beings seem to have held only minor importance compared with the living presence of the local spirits with whom they interacted on a daily basis and sometimes even merged. When we look at those ancient written texts, however, we see something profoundly different. Terrifying gods rule human fate and demand worship, obedience, and often the sacrifice of animals or even humans. People related to the spirits of the enchanted garden as they might to any of the other beings with whom they shared their magical world, but the relationship between these new gods and their people was more one of master and slave.

Since even the most ancient texts depict a time when the gods ruled the religious landscape, they tell us little about how or why this remarkable transformation took place. It may seem we're at an impasse, but the archaeological record gives us a pretty good idea of what happened. The goddess-worshiping cultures of old Europe were apparently destroyed by waves of invasions by warlike pastoralists (nomadic people who herd flocks of animals) who worshiped a pantheon ruled by male gods. In other cases, it seems that early farming societies transformed from within as they gradually developed more and more social inequality. Among nomadic foragers, there are no rich people and no poor people. Possessions are few and limited to what can be carried on one's back. The idea that a person could "own" the natural landscape upon which all their lives depended was entirely foreign. But as agriculture became more and more productive, the wealth of those who controlled fertile lands grew and with it the poverty of others. The first human villagers, like their nomadic forebears, probably had no formal political leadership. But as village life became more complex, they came to select a single person—a chief or headman—to be their political leader. At first, the power of the chief probably depended on the consent of the other villagers, and it was not necessarily correlated with greater wealth or comfort. But over time, the status of the chief tended to become more hereditary, and the inequalities between individuals and clans grew. A similar transformation seems to have taken place among the pastoralists, although their wealth depended on how many animals they owned rather than their landholdings.

With the coming of such technological innovations as irrigation and use of the plow, the inequality between the genders increased along with the inequalities in wealth and power. Men took over control of agricultural activities, warfare became increasingly necessary to defend fertile lands, and patriarchy rose with a vengeance. Although the particulars vary, all the complex agricultural societies that survived into the modern era subordinate women to the authority of men.

Male power is built into their cultural attitudes and their social order, and enforced with the threat of violence and ostracism. The records of the earliest known legal codes, which come from the ancient Middle East, show that the father ruled over the family with an iron grip. He had complete legal power over the women and children and could even give them as slaves to pay off a debt.

Just as men gained power and authority over women, small elites gained power and authority over the mass of average people. Those tribal chiefs were eventually replaced by powerful kings at the head of a large state apparatus. The kings were sometimes considered to be gods themselves or at least to have a divine connection to the gods that obliged them to interpret and carry out their will. At the same time, the first institutionalized religions took to the stage with their priests, temples, and sacrificial rites.

How did average people relate to the powerful new gods described in those texts and in whose name they were ruled? To answer that question, we must take a step back and examine an often overlooked transformation that may be the most fundamental of all—our progressive alienation from the natural world and the spiritual roots of our species. It was, of course, most extreme among those who dwelled in the newly emergent cities that were the cultural and political nerve centers of ancient civilization, but the same process was occurring among the vast majority of people who still lived on the land. As time went by, people came to live in larger and larger villages carved out of the natural landscape, and to work land stripped of its natural vegetation, divided into the rectangular fields best suited for use of the plow, and planted with a single crop. When things went well, there was a vast abundance of food, but this human-created ecosystem had none of the diversity that provides stability to the natural world, and changes in rainfall and average temperature, plagues of insects, or declines in the fertility of the soil easily spelled disaster. And on the human side, there was the ongoing threat from the warlike pastoralists who lived on the borders of most agricultural societies and the constant fear of the often fatal consequences of displeasing the king or the local landlord. In short, fear and insecurity became the new norm for most people, and it was projected onto their gods and the priests and kings who executed their will.

The first human civilizations grew on the fertile alluvial plain around the Tigris and Euphrates Rivers in the region known as Mesopotamia, and their artworks and their myths reflected these primal fears. One of the most famous examples are two nearly five-thousand-year-old Sumerian sculptures discovered in the ruins of the Tell Asmar temple (see Figure 3.2). They depict a woman and a man who are apparently praying, but their most striking feature is their eyes, which are as big as saucers and filled with dread.

There is an ancient Mesopotamian creation myth that spells out the relationship between humans and gods. The great God Enlil created the initial division of the world by separating the heavens

Figure 3.2 *Sumerian praying sculptures from Tell Asmar, Iraq. Early Dynastic period, c. 2800-2400 BCE. Neuroforever, Wikimedia Commons, CC BY-SA 4.0 License.*

from the earth and the waters under the ground. Enlil put his many children, the lesser gods, to work carrying out the arduous work of irrigated agriculture so the gods could be fed, but they eventually got tired of the endless toil and rose up in rebellion. Enki, the god of the waters of earth and among the most clever of gods, suggested that Enlil create humans to do the work. So Enlil killed one of the lesser gods, mixed his blood with clay, and created humans to labor in the fields. At first everything went well. The humans took over the work of the gods and began to flourish. But their growing numbers soon became too noisy for Enlil and he couldn't sleep, so he sent a plague to wipe them out. The wise man Attrahasis went to Enki to plead for help, and Enki suggested that the humans be more quiet and make more offerings to the gods, and when they did, the plague ended. When the humans annoyed the great Enlil a second time, he sent a drought, but Attrahasis persuaded Enki to intervene again, and again Enlil spared the humans. The third time Enlil became so enraged he set a great flood to wipe out every single human. But fortunately for our species, Enki warned Attrahasis in advance and advised him to build a great boat and load it with every kind of animal to ride out the flood. When Enlil discovered what Enki had done, he was furious, but in the meantime the gods had run out of food and Enlil realized the usefulness of humans and allowed them to resettle the earth once again. Thus, the ancient Mesopotamians believed that humans were made to be slaves of the gods and were tolerated only because of their usefulness. And that was far more than a metaphor, for every farmer was required to spend a good portion of each year in forced labor building the irrigation systems and temples the gods and their earthly representatives demanded.

If we look at the most ancient Sumerian texts, it's easy to see the legacy of the Great Goddess where Tara finds her roots. Many of the most powerful and important figures of the Sumerian pantheon were female, and the one that leaps out to us most clearly is the great Inanna. She is certainly the heir of the Great Goddess of earlier times, but she was transformed by the growth of hierarchical society. Inanna was the "Queen of Heaven and Earth," and she reigned as sovereign over all the natural world, but the people of the goddess cultures knew nothing of queens or kings. The primal Goddess did not rule over nature; she *was* nature—its living embodiment with no separation between them. Inanna differed from the primal Goddess in other ways as well. Although she was clearly associated with the fertility of the land (her name originally referred to the fruit of the date palm), she is never shown pregnant, giving birth, or nursing. Archaeologists have found male figurines among the ruins of the goddess cultures, but they are few and far between, and it's obvious they played only a secondary role as consorts and fructifiers. The importance of the primal Goddess was unrivaled. Inanna, on the other hand, was one of a pantheon of powerful deities, and while she was often considered the greatest and most powerful of the gods, she had many rivals for that title.

In one famous myth, the imperious goddess had to wrestle the *me* (powers of civilization) away from her father. According to the story recorded on ancient Sumerian tablets, one day Inanna placed a crown on her head, leaned against an apple tree, and began rejoicing at her femininity: "When she leaned against the apple tree, her vulva was wondrous to behold. Rejoicing at her wondrous vulva, the young woman Inanna applauded herself. She said: 'I Queen of Heaven, shall visit the God of Wisdom [Enki].'"[3]

Inanna set sail on the Boat of Heaven, and when she arrived at Enki's shrine, he gave her cold water to drink, butter cakes to eat, and beer to drink. As they drank more and more beer, they began toasting each other. Enki, swaying with drink, raised his glass and toasted Inanna fourteen times, giving her more and more *me*, including godship, the throne of kingship, the power of decision making and judging, the arts of song and the crafts, and the power of slanderous speech, adoring speech, treachery, and straightforwardness. When the dinner was over, Inanna gathered all her *me,* loaded them onto the Boat of Heaven, and sailed for home.

When Enki sobered up and realized he had given away his powers, he sent his servant Isimud and a group of magical creatures to intercept Inanna and bring his *me* back. When Isimud reached Inanna and made his lord's demands, Inanna was enraged, screaming that he had deceived her and broken his word. Just as Inanna finished these words, Enki's wild-haired creatures seized the Boat of Heaven. Inanna called on her servant Ninshubur who sliced the air with her hand and uttered an earth-shattering cry that sent the magical creatures hurtling away.

Four more times Enki sent horrible monsters against Innana and Ninshubur, and each time Ninshubur defeated them. When Inanna finally reached her home city of Uruk, she declared a festival, and amid her people's rejoicing, she brought the *me* into the city's shrine. The story ends with Enki accepting his defeat and declaring that the *me* can stay in Uruk.

One of Inanna's early epithets was the "lady of the date palms," and like so many goddesses she is associated with fertility and the abundance of the land—a fertility that is also associated with a ravenous sexuality. One hymn to Inanna speaks of her meeting with Dumuzi—a figure sometimes described as her brother and sometimes as her lover. In the midday heat, she kneels by an apple tree, and when Dumuzi approaches she pours out legumes and grain from her womb. In another hymn, Dumuzi tells her that her breast is her field which pours out plants and grain, bread, and water. Dumuzi tells her to pour them out for him, and he will drink all she offers.

Inanna's longing for Dumuzi and their great love is celebrated in countless hymns. In one, she calls Dumuzi's sister up into her bedroom and moans about him until she falls into shaking and trembling. In another, she exclaims that her vulva is full of eagerness like the young moon, but wonders "Who will plow my vulva? Who will plow my wet ground?" Dumuzi answers that he, the king, will plow her vulva, and she responds "Plow my vulva, man of my heart, plow my vulva!"

The reenactment of the sacred marriage of Inanna and Dumuzi was a key part of her cult that not only promoted the fertility of the land, but granted legitimacy to the king who participated in it. It seems the rulers of all the great Mesopotamian cities would engage in this ritual with the king playing the part of Dumuzi and a high priestess as Inanna. Thereafter, the king would be referred to as the consort of Inanna who could bring her fertility and abundance to the people. Thus, the priest reworked the ancient myths and put the power of the Great Goddess to work to justify the rule of the patriarchal king.

To be clear, the marriage of Inanna and Dumuzi was nothing like the ideal patriarchal marriage celebrated in many later myths. Inanna was clearly the Queen and Dumuzi only the consort. This is most obvious in the famous story of Inanna's descent into the underworld. In this myth, Inanna decides she will visit the underworld of death ruled over by her sister, Ereshkigal. As she passes each of the seven gates of the underworld, she is forced to strip off one after another of her magical charms until she is defenseless. She is then struck dead by Ereshkigal and her body hung on a hook. Ninshubur once again comes to the rescue and persuades Enki to help, and Enki creates two magical creatures who descend into the underworld, ingratiate themselves to Ereshkigal, and are rewarded with Inanna's body. They sprinkle the water of life Enki had given them on her body and bring her back to life. As Inanna begins to leave, the judge of the underworld tells her that the law requires someone take her place. As she starts her ascent, demons from the underworld cling to her sides. When she reaches home, the demons try to seize a number of different people and drag them into the underworld as her replacement. But because they were all dressed in mourning for Inanna and they humbly begged for her mercy, she would not let the demons take them. Then the demons came for Dumuzi. He was sitting on a magnificent throne and did not bow to Inanna or ask for her mercy. Inanna was furious. She stared at Dumuzi with the "eye of death," and ordered the demons to take him away.[4]

Given her lusty and wrathful nature, it's no surprise that as warfare grew more and more common in Mesopotamia, Inanna became its goddess. She was proud, restless, and uncontrollable, and she brought storms, earthquakes, and blazing temperatures, and thrived in the heat of battle. One ancient text put it this way:

> Proud Queen of Earth Gods, Supreme among the Heaven Gods,
> Loud Thundering Storm, you pour your rain over all the lands and all the people.
> You make the heavens tremble and the earth quake.
> Great Priestess, who can soothe your troubled heart?
> You flash like lightning over the highlands, you throw your firebrand across the earth.
> Your deafening command, whistling like the South Wind, splits apart great mountains.
> You trample the disobedient like a wild bull; heaven and earth tremble.
> Holy Priestess, who can soothe your troubled heart?[5]

In Sumer, battle itself was known as the "Dance of Inanna," and it was in the fury, fear, and slaughter that her presence was most forcefully known. In one ancient text she says:

When I stand in the front of battle
I am the leader of all lands.
When I stand at the opening of battle,
I am the quiver ready to hand,
When I stand in the midst of the battle,
I am the heart of the battle,
the arm of the warriors,
When I begin moving at the end of the battle,
I am an evilly rising flood[6]

As patriarchal culture grew ever stronger, the popularity of all powerful goddesses like Inanna declined and their functions were often taken by male gods or divided among a variety of goddesses who were subordinated to their male superiors. In the earliest Sumerian myths, the creator of the world was female—Nammu, the goddess of the sea. After fierce Semitic invaders swept up from the deserts to the south and conquered the Sumerians, this myth was recast. The great female creator was destroyed, and the world was subjugated to male authority. In the *Enuma Elish*, the Babylonian creation myth, Nammu was renamed Tiamut and this time the story begins with Tiamut resting in uroboric unity with her male partner, Apsu. They produced many gods as their children, but those gods became so unruly that Apsu decided to destroy them. When he failed, he was murdered by the god Ea and his supporters. Tiamut was enraged, and she created a horde of monsters led by her new consort to destroy the offenders. Her opponents chose Ea's son Marduk as their champion, and after a fierce battle, he cleaved Tiamut's head open with an axe and created the heavens and the earth from her body. From that time on, Marduk reigned as the king of the gods.

***

Since then a supreme male god ruled over antiquity in one form or another and his power continues on in today's monotheistic religions. It was the Greeks, whose literary and philosophic skill far surpassed those of their predecessors who left us the most vivid tales of his exploits. They called him Zeus, and as in many other pantheons, he was a god of the sky and thunder who reigned over the other gods as their king.

Zeus was often shown wielding a thunderbolt with a heavily muscled, youthful physique, but he also had a thick beard and the face of an older man (see Figure 3.3). These days we often associate religion with codes of morality and ethics, but that was hardly the case with the cult of Zeus. He was often vicious and vindictive and seemed to revel in breaking the rules. Various myths hold that he imprisoned his father, was so promiscuous that he had sex with his two sisters and his mother, raped numerous women both divine and human, and even ate his pregnant wife when he came to see the child she carried as a potential threat to his power.

Why would the Greeks worship such a flawed figure? There are countless answers, but at least one is that he seems to have represented their ideal of the patriarchal father. All the gods, even those to whom he was not related, called him father. Although he could be wise and just, he was just as likely to be cruel and destructive. He was worshiped for his sheer ferocity and strength, not his goodness, and he embodied the idea that a dominant male could do whatever he liked to whomever he liked, as long as he was the strongest.

Not all the gods were as powerful or frightening as Zeus. The ancient world had vast pantheons of deities who gained and lost popularity over time. Some died out and faded from memory, while others flourished and spread from one culture to another—often changing names as they went. Most of the lesser gods never made it into the historical record, and we know little about them or the folk

Figure 3.3 *Zeus with thunderbolt, ca. 1686 by Pierre Granier, Louvre, France.*

practices of most common people. As with our hunting and gathering ancestors, the best way to understand these folk practices may be to look at our contemporaries who practice similar religions.

It is sometimes said that Hinduism, today's largest polytheistic faith, has 33 million deities, but whatever the actual number, it seems likely that the religious beliefs of the ancient world were just as diverse. Every Indian village has its own protective deity, and unlike the male deities who rule the pantheon, the village deities are often pictured as nurturing females who are a source of support in times of trouble. The numerous festivals and celebrations dedicated to them and to the more powerful gods are a source of joy and communal spirit that help cement social relations in the village. In many ancient societies, families and clans had their own ancestral deities as well, and each group had their unique forms of worship.

The primal Goddess seems to have survived in the form of these local deities and in more powerful goddesses who specialized in such matters as fertility or love. And she reemerged from time to time as the Great Goddess who, at least among her followers, displaced the male gods as the ruler of the pantheon. The great Egyptian goddess Isis is a case in point. She began as a classic mother goddess and her love of and fidelity to her husband was central to her cult, but she evolved into something much more than that. Isis's defining myth tells of the way her love and sheer determination brought her husband, Osiris, back from the dead after he was murdered by his brother. After her son, Horus, was born, she showed him the same loving care, hiding him from Osiris's brother until he was old enough to avenge his father and claim the throne of Egypt.

Great myths are always filled with drama, and beneath the surface are layers upon layers of symbolism and meaning. In terms of the natural world, Osiris's life, slaying, and rebirth represent the rhythms of the seasons—the crops that grow in the fields, are cut down, and born again the next spring. Although the crops were seen as the body of Osiris, it was Isis's love and heroic efforts that brought them to life. The incredible fertility of the Nile basin that was home to the Egyptian people was completely dependent on the seasonal flooding of their great river, and the reason it flooded were the tears Isis shed for her dead Osiris.

Like so many of the myths recorded by the ancient scribes, this one is as much about the political world as the natural one, and it is there its greatest import may lie. In Egyptian cosmology, the pharaoh was far more than just a political leader. His sublime presence engendered bounty, well-being, and order. He was not a mere representative of the divine, he *was* the divine—a living god—and as long as he was vigorous and strong, Egypt prospered. But as effective as it was in legitimizing the vast power of the pharaoh, such an ideology had an obvious problem. The gods were immortal, and all the ritual, pomp, and ceremony surrounding the pharaoh couldn't hide the fact that he grew old and died.

The solution was, of course, to grant the pharaoh mythical immortality in the land of the dead through the mysterious process of mummification. The death of a pharaoh was equated with the death of Osiris, and the birth of the next pharaoh with that of Horus, his son. It was, moreover, only through the love and magical power of Isis that the divine essence of the pharaoh was preserved and passed on to his successor. Once again, the power of the Great Goddess is appropriated to serve the patriarchal king.

Isis's role in the cult that deified the pharaoh and ensured his immortality was, of course, far removed from the common people. To them, she was the exemplar of wifely devotion and maternal love. She was associated with Hathor, the Egyptian goddess of sex and love, and with Venus (Aphrodite) in the Roman world, and she was also seen to be the embodiment of the mysterious force that attracted women and men to each other. Her passion was, however, almost always expressed within the faithful confines of conventional marriage. In fact, some myths say she actually *founded* the institution of marriage. Marriage proposals were often made at her temples where she served as a witness to the lover's vows, thereby making them binding.

When Egypt finally fell to Roman conquest, Isis leapt the bounds of her traditional home, shed her association with the cult of the pharaohs, and spread throughout the empire. Her cult became so popular that it was the primary challenger to Christianity in the early centuries of the Common Era. The reasons for her popularity aren't hard to find. While the Olympic gods of the Greeks and Romans were often aloof and indifferent to human affairs, Isis was referred to as "the one who listens." She had a passionate concern for the welfare of her followers, and like Tara was always ready to come to their aid whether they needed wealth, protection, or good health. "Isis toiled without rest on behalf of her beloved human family, sheltering them on land and sea, banishing the storms that beset their lives, and stretching out to them a strong right hand of a Savior."[7]

In Egypt, Isis's power was always shared with other gods, but her Roman followers came to see her as the underlying power, the divine essence, of all the gods. The only Roman novel to survive in its entirety, Apuleius's *Metamorphoses*, leaves no doubt about her supreme power. At the conclusion of the novel, Isis saves the protagonist from the dire consequences of his failed attempts at magic, and appears to him in all her divine glory saying:

> You see me here, Lucius, in answer to your prayer. I am Nature, the universal Mother, mistress of all the elements, primordial child of time, sovereign of all things spiritual, queen of the dead, queen also of the immortals, the single manifestation of all gods and goddesses that are. My nod governs the shining heights of Heaven, the wholesome sea-breezes, the lamentable silences of the world below. Though I am worshipped in many aspects, known by countless names, and propitiated with all manner of different rites, yet the whole round earth venerates me … Some know me as Juno, some as Bellona … others as Hecate, others again as Rhamnubia, but … the Egyptians who excel in ancient learning and worship me with ceremonies proper to my godhead, call me by my true name, namely, Queen Isis.[8]

The One God

It is often the small societies on the fringes of the main cultural centers that give birth to the most profound new innovations, and that was certainly true of the ancient Hebrews. Although a great deal of attention has been focused on the growth of monotheism among the Hebrews, in some ways it was not as radical a development as it seems. It was common for the people of the ancient Middle East to believe that the god of their city or clan was the most powerful of all gods. So, it wasn't that big a leap from the belief in a great god who ruled over all the others, to a belief that he or she was the one true god and that all others were false. In fact, the Egyptian pharaoh Akhenaten proclaimed Aten, the sun god, to be the one true god, centuries before Hebrew monotheism was fully developed. After his death, however, Akhenaten's reforms were quickly undone by the priestly caste of Egypt, and they seemed to have little lasting impact. Yahweh (the Hebrew name of God revealed to Moses), on the other hand, took centuries to evolve from a tribal deity who demanded the exclusive allegiance of his people to the single God of all the universe, but it was a vision that was to have a far more profound effect on the world.

It wasn't just monotheism itself, but the type of monotheism that the Hebrews developed that was so game-changing. As we have seen, at the dawn of the gods, the most important deities were probably female. But the further we move from small-scale farming communities to the patriarchal hierarchy of agricultural civilizations, the more dominant the male gods became. The monotheism of the Hebrews, however, went to far greater extremes, entirely eliminating all the female gods and leaving only the single male figure of "God the Father." This was a truly revolutionary development. Even though the agricultural peoples did grow increasingly distant from the natural environment, they always recognized their dependence on the cycles of nature and the fertility of the earth and sky. Even when the goddesses were pushed aside, male gods took over their symbolic connection to nature. The solitary male God of the Hebrews, on the other hand, struck down all imagery but His own, gave humankind dominion over the natural world, and ordained that they rule over it. Their only dependence was to be on Him, not the forces of nature or the gods who symbolized its power.

Another striking feature of Hebrew monotheism was its hegemonic claim to be the one true faith. The gods of polytheistic pantheons were often in competition with each other, and while the followers of one deity may have claimed her to be the most powerful of all the gods, they did not deny the legitimacy of other gods and their practices. Even before the development of absolute monotheism, the God of the Hebrews condemned the worship of any other gods, and His followers were ruthless in executing His demands. The Hebrew bible gives us an account of what may have been the first religious pogrom in recorded history. It tells us that when Moses returned from the mountain where he received God's ten commandments, he discovered that some of the people he left behind had made an image of a golden calf and began to worship it. Moses called his followers before him and said:

> Thus says the Lord, the God of Israel, "Put your sword on your side each of you! Go back and forth from gate to gate throughout the camp, and each of you kill your brother, your friend, and your neighbor!" The sons of Levi did as Moses commanded, and about three thousand of the people fell on that day. Moses said, "Today you have ordained yourselves for the service of the Lord, each one at the cost of a son or a brother, and so have brought a blessing on yourselves this day."[9]

Many contemporary scholars doubt that Moses was a historical person, but even if this story is pure myth, it is a striking illustration of a new and powerful exclusivity. This early zealotry was limited to a fairly small area, but as new forms of monotheism spread out from these roots, they brought a legacy of intolerance with them. The various monotheistic faiths with their roots in the Hebraic tradition fought bitter battles among themselves, and viciously repressed the faith of their polytheistic predecessors. Their most virulent attacks were often directed at those who pursued the ecstatic states that were so much a part of primal spirituality. Those who practiced traditional shamanism and many who merely participated in orgasmic rituals or celebrations, were condemned as Satanists and degenerates, and often met a grizzly fate.

Another key piece of the monotheistic puzzle, and certainly a far more positive one, was the belief in universal ethics. Today we think of religion and morality as intimately related, but that was not the case in the ancient world. Seen by today's standards, the gods, like the kings of the ancient world, acted with a shocking amorality that was free from the ethical restraints that bound common people. Moreover, even when adhered to the ethical norms of that era were far different from our own. There were strict obligations to support and protect one's kin, but outsiders could be abused, enslaved, or even killed with impunity. The logic of monotheism, however, lead in a different direction. Since there is only one God and we are all His people, the same rules apply to everyone, and the Hebrew God made that clear again and again.

The God of the Hebrews was certainly terrifying, but He was also loving and just—a deity who was involved in the lives of His people and wished them to flourish. Indeed, the Christians put such a strong emphasis on God's love that it came to be seen as one of His defining characteristics. The ethical prohibitions ensconced in universal rules thus came to be supplemented by more positive virtues such as kindness, generosity, and concern for others.

As Christianity rose to power in the Roman Empire, the cults of Isis and the other traditional gods met with increasing repression. The religious free-for-all of the ancient world was replaced with an ever-increasing demand to conform to Christian orthodoxy and accept the one male God. The temples of gods and goddesses were closed or converted to churches, and women were forbidden to perform priestly roles in the new religion.

Although the Christians succeeded in crushing the cult of Isis, the Great Goddess was soon to reemerge in other forms, most notably in the cult of the Virgin Mary. Mary's role in the New Testament was only as the mother of Jesus. She was a holy woman chosen by God to bear his son, but she had no special powers or divine importance of her own. But as one of the few female figures in the new patriarchal religious landscape, she became the object of ever-increasing devotion. Her followers were soon calling on her for help and salvation in much the same way as they had called on Isis. Mary was always depicted as tenderhearted, compassionate, and merciful—willing to help with whatever was needed: healing the sick, protection from disasters, childbearing, or cleansing a sin.

The church hierarchy viewed Mary with ambivalence. The kind of passionate devotion she instilled in her followers was vital to the church's success, but that very fervor seemed, at times, to threaten the place of Jesus and the Father God at the top of the Christian hierarchy. It was to Mary, not Jesus, that many common Christians turned in times of distress. The theological response to this dilemma was complex, but in essence the church revered Mary, but made it clear that she was only an intermediary and that the true power was the male God's alone. Mary could intercede on behalf of troubled souls, bring their petitions to her son, and even plead their case, but the final outcome was up to Him. Jesus was both man and God, but however revered, Mary was only human. And it was her very humanity that made her so approachable and loved. In a sense, Mary was like the church itself, standing between man and god as a loving intercessor. She was set apart and above other humans, but in no sense a goddess, herself.

Another striking difference between Mary and figures like Isis and Sita is that Mary never played the part of the ideal wife. That may seem surprising in light of the overwhelming importance of that role in patriarchal culture, but the centrality given to Mary's virginity made that impossible. Many early Christians considered sex to be base and defiling—something that was only allowed within the confines of marriage and, even better, done without. Although the ancient myths were full of stories of mortals having sex with the gods, Mary's miracle was to conceive a child with no sex at all.

The historical Mary may have had other children aside from Jesus, but the Virgin Mary is never shown with any other children. Not only was she never depicted as having sexual desire, even sex with her husband would have been a violation of her holy purity. Thus, the Virgin Mary could never be a model for women who must perform the "wifely function" required for procreation. She was, however, an exemplar of another value of the patriarchy—female chastity. Over the years, the example of the Holy Virgin certainly helped countless girls defend their chastity against any violation that would ruin their reputation and with it their chances of marriage and childbearing—a woman's greatest source of worth in patriarchal culture.

Despite her chastity, Mary's role as the "Mother of God" holds a deep resonance with the great mother goddesses that preceded her. Apparitions of the Virgin Mary have come to countless people around the world, but none were historically more important or make the connection to the ancient goddesses more clear, than the visions of a simple peasant, Juan Diego in the Spanish colony that was to become the state of Mexico. Because the apparition he saw, known as the Virgin of Guadalupe, had brown skin and spoke Nahuatl, the traditional language of the Aztec Empire, she was a powerful force in cementing the Catholic faith among the conquered people of the New World. To this day, the basilica built on the site of Juan Diego's great vision is the most popular destination of Catholic pilgrimage in the world. Most interesting for our purposes is the fact that the Virgin first appeared to Juan Diego standing in the midst of a giant maguey cactus—a plant that was traditionally associated with the Aztec fertility goddess, Mayahuel, who like Mary provided maternal support and nourishment for those who called upon her.

Although Mary was often confined within the bounds of patriarchal culture and church hierarchy, the power of her awakened femininity broke through again and again, and she is in many ways the heart and soul of Catholic spirituality. The great twentieth-century mystic Thomas Merton, gives us a taste of what Mary means to so many contemporary Catholics:

> The glory of Mary is purely and simply the glory of God in her, and she, like anyone else, can say that she has nothing that she has not received from Him through Christ .... It is because she is, of all the saints, the most perfectly poor and the most perfectly hidden, the one who has absolutely nothing whatever that she attempts to possess as her own, that she can most fully communicate to the rest of us the grace of the infinitely selfless God. ... all our sanctity depends on her maternal love. The ones she desires to share the joy of her own poverty and simplicity, the ones whom she wills to be hidden as she is hidden, are the ones who share her closeness to God.[10]

Theistic Spirituality

In the beginning, the gods were just new residents in the enchanted garden of the natural world. The primal spiritual connection to the mysteries of the rivers, mountains, and lakes, to the earth, the animals, and the countless other magical beings that filled the world was not broken for millennia to come. The new gods brought their distinctive religious practices, but they were overlaid upon the abundance of primal spirituality. It was not until the advent of hegemonic monotheism that the religious balance would shift.

Right from the beginning, the most important forms of theistic spiritual practice were worship and prayer. This prayer to Ishtar (the Babylonian name for Inanna), inscribed on ancient cuneiform tablets, sounds much like what can be heard in a modern-day church:

> Gracious Ishtar who rules over the universe,
> heroic Ishtar, who creates humankind,
> who walks before the cattle, who loves the shepherd
> You give justice to the distressed, the suffering you give them justice …
>
> Where you cast your glance, the dead awaken, the sick arise;
> The bewildered beholding you face find the right way.
> I appeal to you miserable and distraught,
> tortured by pain, your servant,
> be merciful and hear by prayer!
> I await you my mistress; my soul turns toward you.
> I beseech you: relieve my plight.[11]

It is said that to our primal ancestors, the whole world was a church, but with the coming of the gods came temples and priests performing increasingly elaborate rituals. They sought to confine the sense of awe engendered by the boundless wonders of the enchanted garden to a few holy places and religious events. Ceremonies and celebrations led by the priestly caste often displaced the spontaneous singing and dancing of traditional tribal groups, and as new religious elites asserted their control, average people often became spectators rather than autonomous agents of their religious lives.

In primal societies, the highest form of religious experience was to merge with one of the powerful beings and thereby gain access to their power and patronage. In the polytheistic traditions, the picture was more mixed; but in all the holy books of Western monotheism, God was overwhelmingly powerful and distant, and those who came into His presence were struck with what the great Lutheran theologian Rudolph Otto described as terror (*tremendum*) and fascination (*fascinans*). When Moses heard God's voice coming from the burning bush, he turned his face away and could not look. The prophet Ezekiel was so overcome by his great vision of the chariot of God that he literally fell on his face. As the prophet Amos put it:

> The lion roars, who can help feeling afraid?
> The Lord Yahweh speaks, who can refuse to prophesy?[12]

That was certainly the way the prophet Mohammad felt when, one night during Ramadan, he was torn from his sleep by a devastating divine presence. An angel of God appeared to him and gave him a single command: "Recite!" Mohammad refused and protested that he was not a *kahin,* one of the disreputable soothsayers of Arabia who are believed to be possessed by a *jinni* (spirit). The angel seized Mohammad in its crushing grip, and when Mohammad could stand it no longer, he released him and demanded once again "Recite!" Mohammed again refused and again the angel took him in his overwhelming embrace and repeated his demand. Only after his third terrifying encounter did Mohammad relent and allow the first divine words of a new scripture to pour from his lips.

Mohammad reacted with horror to this whole event, and fearing that he had become a *kabin* himself, decided to throw himself off a mountain. But on his way up the mountainside, he heard another divine voice telling him he was a prophet of God, and when he looked up, he saw the angel Gabriel in the form of a man astride the horizon. There was no escape from the terrifying vision, for even when Mohammad turned his head, the angel was visible in every direction.[13]

The stark contrast between the experience of the shaman and the other virtuosos of primal spirituality, and that of the prophets can, of course, be partly explained by the vastly different religions traditions that surrounded them. But they also reflect a profound psychological difference. We know from the studies of the nomadic foragers who survived into the modern era that they were far less individualistic than we are today. They defined themselves in terms of the groups they belonged to and the places they lived, not their personal characteristics. Their boundaries of self were far more permeable and vaguely defined. People merged into animals and animals into people. The trees, streams, and mountains were all alive, and the powerful beings were a natural part of the environment. As we evolved more complex and hierarchical social systems, individualism became ever more pronounced. Sharp boundaries were created between self and other, and enormous psychic energy was devoted to protecting and maintaining the individual ego. Thus, an encounter with a deity that was so incredibly powerful and so completely other posed a terrifying threat—not so much to physical safety but to the survival of the ego. The only hope was complete surrender and submission to the will of God. Indeed, the very meaning of the word Islam is "to submit."

Some traditions within the vast array of Western monotheism came to soften this terrifying view of God, instead emphasizing His love and approachability and sometimes even resurrecting elements of the earlier ecstatic practices. Numerous Protestant sects carried on emotional worship services, where the fortunate would have the ecstatic experience of being touched by the Holy Spirit of God. The Sufi mystics of the Islamic tradition sometimes described their longing for God as one might describe the longing for a long-lost lover, just as Catholic nuns were often described as brides of Christ. St. Francis heard God in the birds who spoke to him, and the charismatic founder of Hasidism, the Baal Shem Tov, had his deepest connection to God while dancing in the forests.

A very different relationship with the divine that intimates a more transpersonal self-emerged in India around the same time the great Hebrew prophets were bringing their message into the world. The Indian polytheists posited a great divine essence known as Brahman that underlies all existence and from which everything arises—even the gods themselves. In whatever tradition, attempts to describe this ultimate often begin by saying that it is completely beyond conceptual understanding and cannot be captured by words, but nonetheless go on to describe it as such things as unborn, undying, luminous, or the origin of all things. But what is clear is that Brahman was not some distant, fearful being, but our deepest, true nature. As Krishna tells Arjuna in the most famous phrase from the great Hindu classic, the Bhagavad Gita, "*Tat Tvam Asi*" (Thou Art That). Far from instigating a terrifying awe, the union of the individual soul with Brahman was described in terms of bliss, joy, and peace.

As time went on, the idea of God as a transcendental ultimate present within each of us became more popular in the monotheistic religions as well, but there was a problem. The Hindu polytheists had no trouble envisioning a vast array of personal gods to whom people could pray for divine assistance, while at the same time positing a great universal divine that was the source of them all. That option was not, however, available to the monotheists, and there was always a tension between the personal God of the scriptures and of popular belief and the transcendent God favored by intellectuals and mystics. Even the Koran, which presents the least personalistic view of God of the three great monotheistic traditions, still describes Him as having such human characteristics as being gracious, merciful, sovereign, wise, and patient. Nonetheless, it strikes me how mystics in the monotheistic and the polytheistic religions alike still report the experience of dissolution into an ultimate beyond all description or understanding. Even in the Eastern religions, however, this kind of spirituality is only for the few. For the majority of people, theistic spirituality, whether monotheistic or polytheistic, is still a way of relating to something external and outside the self. Whether one worships a deity, prays for help and guidance, or offers up sacrifices and tribute, the impassable barrier remains.

Sources

By far the best source on the "goddess cultures" of preliterate Europe and the Near East is the work of Marija Gimbutas. She was a professor of European Archaeology at UCLA for many years, and she not only provides the most convincing analysis of the archaeological evidence, she actually did many of the important archaeological excavations of these sites herself. I relied most heavily on her final work, *The Living Goddesses* (Berkeley: University of California Press, 1999).

For the goddesses of recorded history, my favorite source was the scholarly and balanced work of David Kinsley, particularly *The Goddesses' Mirror: Visions of the Divine from East and West* (Albany:

State University of New York Press, 1989). Joseph Campbell's *Goddesses: Mysteries of the Feminine Divine* (Novato, CA: New World Library, 2013) was also very useful. As arguably the first great goddess of recorded history, I gave Inanna some special attention, and there is no better work on her than the wonderful collaborative translation by the folklorist, Diane Wolkstein, and the cuneiformist, Samuel Noah Kramer, in their book *Inanna: Queen of Heaven and Earth, Her Stories and Hymns from Sumer* (New York: Harper & Row, 1983).

Once again, the works of Max Weber, Robert Bellah, and Huston Smith were central to understanding the sociological forces that brought the coming of the gods and what that meant to average people. Raymond Firth's *We the Tilopia: A Sociological Study of Kinship in Primitive Polynesia* (New York: American Book Company, 1936) is a fascinating study of a traditional society almost completely isolated from the modern world that shows the relationship between an early form of kingship and the gods. The analysis of monotheistic spirituality is mostly my own, and I take full responsibility for any of its shortcomings.

4

The Disenchanted World

The magic has gone. The enchanted garden of our ancestors has been lost, and the world has become a cold and indifferent place. Instead of the vast living mystery our forbearers inhabited, it seems today's world is only configurations of matter and energy interacting on the basis of objective laws. The animals who were once our sacred kin are now nothing more than food or entertainment, and we deny the sentience of the trees, the rivers, and the earth. Even consciousness itself is seen as nothing more than an epiphenomenon of the physical processes of our body that is doomed to blink out when they cease.

Of course, I am overstating the case for the old ways of thinking still have surprising resilience, but there is no denying that a profound transformation has taken place that has moved our culture further and further away from Tara and the primal connection to nature that she embodies. It would be easy to lay the responsibility at the feet of the jealous monotheistic God who allows no other gods before Him, but that is only part of the story. The roots of this transformation go back much further to the advent of a new pattern of human thought.

The Axial Breakthrough

This new kind of thinking entered the historical record almost simultaneously in such far-flung places as Greece, India, and China during the first millennium BCE. The German philosopher Karl Jaspers dubbed the period from roughly the eighth to the third centuries BCE the Axial Age. Although there have been endless arguments about how useful a concept that really is, there's little doubt something profound happened. Looking back at that period, it seems the human world did, at least figuratively, turn on its axis. That being said, it may be more fruitful to call it the axial breakthrough, because the first small steps leading up to that momentous change began long before that era, and its consequences continued to unfold long after.

No great breakthroughs in history are the product of a single genius acting alone. Although such names as Confucius, Plato, Mahavira (the founder of Jainism), Socrates, Mencius, Aristotle, and Siddhartha Gautama come to mind as the fathers of this new era, they are all an inseparable part of the vast drama of our social evolution. Of course, the content of their philosophies differed, but for the first time there *were* philosophies. If we look closely, we see that they were all based on a radically new type of thinking that had only been known before in limited domains such as astronomy and metallurgy.

Since the beginning of human language, we always understood our world and our culture through myths, stories, and rituals. Epic myths described the creation of the world and explained the changing seasons, droughts and floods, why we get sick, and how to lead our lives. Shared rituals symbolized and reinforced our social bonds, and stories about the people and events of their lives taught our forebears how they should think and behave. With the axial breakthrough, human thought moved to a new level of abstraction. For the first time, we were able to stand back from our day-to-day world and look at it as if from a distance. Philosophies based on critical thought and systematic analysis challenged the very foundations of our world, and great thinkers demanded radical change. To be sure, people in earlier times would sometimes criticize an unjust ruler or the religious beliefs of those who followed a different god, but until this axial shift, their most basic cultural assumptions went largely unseen and unchallenged.

This new kind of thought presupposed a more individualized ego-dominant personality than in earlier times, so it's no surprise that the new approach spread among the social groups most likely have that kind of orientation—wandering intellectuals, holy men detached from the moorings of kin and community, merchants and traders living by capitalist rules in the midst of traditional agricultural societies, bureaucrats who saw themselves as holders of the virtue that was so lacking in the social order, and the privileged with the leisure time for thought and reflection.

Although all the writers who have explored the axial breakthrough recognize that it occurred in many cultures around the world, they often focus on a single case as the model for the others. Some use the prophetic age of the Hebrews that shaped Western monotheism. While the Hebrew prophets did have the critical perspective on their society that was a trademark of the axial breakthrough, Hebrew thought of that era still focused on myth and narrative, and never broke through to logical systematic theory. The ringing criticisms of the prophets centered almost entirely on the failure of their people and their rulers to live up to the demands of Yahweh, and certainly none of the prophets dared challenge the supremacy of the One God.

The classical Greeks were an entirely different matter. For the purposes of this book, I want to look most closely at the breakthrough in northern India, but it is hard not to be awestruck by the explosion of the intellect that occurred among a handful of Greeks in their small city-states that laid the foundations of Western civilization. Not only did they develop a variety of competing philosophical schools of unprecedented sophistication, they excelled at the art of rhetoric, made major mathematical breakthroughs, laid the foundation for modern science, crafted sculpture of stunning beauty, and even wrote great tragic plays that are still read more than two thousand years later. It is impossible to summarize all their achievements here, but one thing that stands out is not only that they wielded the power of rational systematic thought with surpassing skill, but that they often elevated rational inquiry itself to almost mystical heights. Plato and his numerous followers, for example, believed the best possible form of governance was by the "philosopher king" who had mastered the most subtle forms of thought, and many diverse schools of Greek thought held that it was rational inquiry and deliberation that led to the most profound spiritual insights.

The central concern of the axial breakthrough in ancient China was the nature of a good society and how to create it, and as with the Greeks and the Indians, there was intense intellectual competition among different schools of thought and beliefs. To the Confucianists, the good society was still ruled by an elite, but one based not on blood but on virtue. The "superior man" showed both *jen* (open-hearted humanity), and *li* (propriety). He carried out the right ritual actions, and showed respect and obedience to his superiors and care for his subordinates whether in his patriarchal family or the broader society. In the Confucian view, you should love everyone, but your first concern was always for the members of your own family. Their main intellectual competitors, the Moists, on the other hand, advocated truly universal ethics and the belief that universal love was the key to a good society that overrode all other concerns including the traditional obligations of filial piety. The Taoists represented the more mystical side of Chinese life, and they sought a simple, spontaneous life that followed the way of nature. Unlike any of the other schools in this highly patriarchal society, the Taoists often saw greater virtue in the feminine than the masculine. Chapter 61 of Lao Tzu's timeless classic, *The Way and Its Power,* says that "The female always overcomes the male by tranquility," and chapter 6 holds that:

> The spirit of the valley never dies,
> It is called the subtle and profound female.
> The gate of the subtle and profound female
> Is the root of heaven and earth.
> It is continuous and it seems to be always existing,
> Use it and you will never wear it out.[1]

While these axial cultures looked for ways the wise might improve the outside world, the Indians of this era looked within. The Buddha was the archetypal figure of the Axial Age in India, and it would be hard to imagine a list of the world's greatest thinkers that did not include his name. But Siddhartha Gautama was part of a much larger movement of creative thought and spiritual inquiry throughout the plains of Northern India where the river Ganges flowed. The "seekers" who led this movement lived mostly by begging and needed no institutional connections or high rank, only a charismatic personality and a clear message.

There were popular leaders who taught atheism, those who denied the reality of karma and said nothing was moral or immoral, and those who were strict determinists and denied all free will. There were materialists, agnostics, and atomists. But the three most popular and influential schools—the Buddhists, Jains, and the Brahmanical renunciates who sought a direct spiritual realization beyond the elaborate rituals of their priestly inheritance—clearly had strong areas of agreement. As Geoffrey Samuel puts it: The key component of these teachers' message was:

> the ideal of the renunciation of ordinary life and of the emotions, feelings, impulses that tied one to it, a renunciation that also included rejection of family, descendants and rebirth … The key element was a reversal of everyday life such that the goal of liberation from rebirth came to be the centre around which their lives were now constructed. Following the reversal, the emotional entanglements of everyday life came to be seen as traps and obstacles to the achievement of that goal.[2]

It is hard to overstate how radical a development this was. The idea that a significant proportion of society would reject the everyday world of family and economic responsibility and devote their entire lives to spiritual pursuits would have been unthinkable to our hunting and gathering ancestors, and for that matter even among the early agricultural societies that had the economic surplus to support such pursuits. The fact that Indian society of that time encouraged such single-minded spiritual dedication, and provided the material means to make it possible on such a large scale, was entirely new.

Each of these three dominant schools of Indian thought had their own terminology and philosophy, but their most important differences were probably in their methods. The Brahmanical renunciates and especially the Jains emphasized what can only be called extreme ascetic practices—the Jains actually saw death by starvation as a high holy path—along with some simple meditations on such things as loving kindness and compassion. It was the Buddhists who had the broadest arsenal of meditation techniques which they saw as essential to liberation. Contemporary Western Buddhists often emphasize the fact that the Buddha gave his teachings to laypeople and monks alike, and held that everyone had the potential for liberation. While that is certainly true, it is also true that he believed it was far faster and easier to attain liberation as an ascetic than as a householder. When speaking to laypeople, the Buddha emphasized the importance of ethical behavior and generosity, while his teachings on meditation were usually reserved for the monks. The Buddha was enormously charismatic, and when someone heard his teachings and was inspired to join the community that had gathered around him, he was required to follow a strict ascetic regimen—no sex, no family life, and only one meal a day eaten before noon. He had to give up all his wealth and live by begging, and avoid many of the things average people found joyful—singing, dancing, and even high comfortable beds.

I use the masculine pronoun here, because at least at the start all of the Buddha monastic followers were men. It seems that the Buddha originally resisted the ordination of women, but relented when he heard the pleas of many women, including his own family members who wished to join his *sangha* (the community of monastics). Even after he allowed women to join his sangha, however, they were separated from the men and always strictly subordinated to male authority.

While this ideal of the ascetic who withdraws from all worldly attachments is characteristically Indian, the Indians also shared a predilection toward logical, systematic thought with all the other great axial traditions. Consider the Four Noble Truths that many hold to be the Buddha's first teachings and the core of the Buddhist path. The Buddha begins with the kind of discerning look at the world around him that is typical of the axial thinkers, and concludes that life is full of suffering and discontent. In the second noble truth, he answers the next logical question: What is the cause of this discontent? And his answer is unequivocal: clinging and attachment. We suffer because we cling to things that are impermanent and ever-changing. We suffer because we cling to our desire to be free of everything that afflicts us. The third noble truth is the answer to the next obvious question: Can we end suffering? And he gives us the logical answer: Yes, by ending craving and attachment. The last noble truth answers the culminating question: How then do we do that? By following the Eightfold Noble Path, we are told, and if we look at this path, we see that the Buddha once again makes a clear systematic presentation, this time setting forth the specific things we need to do to cultivate the ethical behavior, wisdom, and meditative awareness necessary to achieve liberation. No modern logician could have come up with a more elegant formulation.

Another critical breakthrough in all the axial societies was the emergence of universal ethics. Of course, people in all times and places have a sense of right and wrong, but their ethics were often particularistic. Rather than following some universal standard that applied to everyone, they looked at family, friends, and kin in a very different way than strangers or those from competing groups. The people of many traditional societies think nothing of abusing, torturing, or even killing those outside the bounds of their group, while at the same time feeling obliged to protect and support those within. Even today, we still make these kinds of particularistic ethical decisions. We bend the rules of fairness to help our own children and are willing to unleash the most frightful military horrors against our enemies, no matter how weak and defenseless they may be. But the ideal promulgated by the axial thinkers, and essential to a just society, is to treat everyone with impartiality and protect all from violence and abuse.

It is clear from ancient texts that the Buddhists and Jains strove tirelessly to promote ethical restraint (not killing, stealing, etc.) as well as such universal virtues as generosity and kindness.[3] The growing power of rationalism and universal ethics was, as Weber pointed out more than a century ago, an important force behind the growth of Western monotheism as well—for a single monotheistic God could do a far better job advancing His moral claims than a cacophony of competing deities. In Asia, they took a different approach by rooting their moral systems in the universal laws of karma that applied to everyone, even the gods. But either way, the growth of trade and international commerce and creation of large empires that contained many diverse ethnic groups required some kind of universal ethical system, and the axial thinkers helped provide it.

The Spirituality of the Axial Breakthrough

The rational, analytic thought so central to the axial breakthrough is often seen as antithetical to the spontaneity of the spiritual life, and in some ways I think that's true. It is, however, the incredible power of rational thought that it can be put to almost any end, including spiritual development. Although one can argue whether formal theology did much to advance genuine spirituality, the roots of theology certainly lie in the axial breakthrough, and many of the ideas most central to our understanding of spiritual life depend upon the critical self-reflection of axial thought.

For example, when the ancient Indians first declared that all things, even the gods, came from Brahman—an ultimate that was without characteristics and beyond all understanding—it was in one sense a rejection of logical thought. At the same time, however, the idea that there is an ultimate ground beyond all ideas and characteristics is itself a sophisticated abstraction that could never have occurred before the axial breakthrough. This idea, moreover, cropped up in the thought of all the axial societies in one place or another.

Here is the opening verse of Lao Tzu's *Tao Te Ching:*

Existence is beyond the power of words
To define:

Terms may be used
But none of them are absolute.
In the beginning of heaven and earth there were no words,
Words came out of the womb of matter;
And whether a man dispassionately
Sees to the core of life
Or passionately
Sees the surface
The core and the surface
Are essentially the same,
Words making them seem different
Only to express appearance.
If name be needed, wonder names them both:
From wonder into wonder
Existence opens.[4]

On the other side of the world, Plotinus, who is held to be the founder of the Neoplatonist philosophy, taught that there is a supreme, totally transcendent "one" containing no division, multiplicity, or distinction; beyond all categories of being and non-being and from which all things derive. Plotinus's ideas were not only enormously influential in the later Roman Empire but also spread from there to Eastern Christianity, Islam, and the European Renaissance.

In addition to allowing such unprecedented subtlety in religious thought, the axial breakthrough also bore another spiritual fruit that is seldom recognized–organized systematic practices for meditation and spiritual development. Deep, spiritual experiences seem to be universal throughout all human cultures, and often appear to occur spontaneously or as the result of a traumatic shock, severe illness, or unexpected encounter. And as we have seen, the cultivation of ecstatic states was also an important part of primal spirituality.

Frenzied drumming and dancing, physical exhaustion, pain, partial asphyxiation, and psychotropic drugs were all used to push the participants beyond the limits of normal psychic functioning and into ecstatic states in which they could enter the realm of the spirits. In India of the Buddha's time, fasting was apparently widely used in this way. During his six years as a wandering "seeker," the Buddha himself fasted until he became so emaciated he could feel his backbone when he pressed his hand on his stomach. As he reached the edge of death, however, he rejected this approach so common to primal spirituality. In his first discourse after he had his great enlightenment experience, he told a small group of followers:

> There are these two extremes that are not to be indulged in by one who has gone forth (become a spiritual seeker). Which two? That which is devoted to sensual pleasure with reference to sensual objects: base, vulgar, common, ignoble, unprofitable; and that which is devoted to self-affliction: painful, ignoble, unprofitable. Avoiding both of these extremes, the middle way realized by the Tathagata—producing vision, producing knowledge—leads to calm, to direct knowledge, to self-awakening, to unbinding (nirvana).[5]

The code of monastic behavior (*Vinaya)* laid down by the Buddha forbids virtually all the traditional techniques of ecstasy, even those that do no harm to the body. Monks were not allowed to sing, dance, drum, become intoxicated, or even have sex.

The condemnation of such wild abandon was hardly limited to the Buddhist, but what is striking about the Buddha's teachings was what he offered instead. He and others among the Jains and Vedantists took the rational self-reflection of the axial breakthrough and applied it to the quest for spiritual liberation, creating something entirely new in the process—a "spiritual technology" that made profound spiritual states available to anyone willing to follow their systematic instructions. It may seem contradictory to take a rational approach to transcend the rational, but the meditation techniques pioneered in axial India have proven their effectiveness for more than two thousand years—being refined and expanded over the centuries so that today there are a vast array of meditation techniques and a sophisticated understanding of their benefits and pitfalls that would have been unthinkable before the axial breakthrough.

The Disenchanted World

This new pattern of rational systematic thought did not replace our myths, stories, and narratives; it merely added a new dimension on top of the old. Millennia after the original axial breakthrough, we still devote far more time to telling stories about ourselves and those around us, and listening to mythic tales about various celebrities, political figures, and fictional characters, than we do in rational reflection. The process of "self-construction" that is so central to our psychology is based on the stories we tell ourselves about who and what we are. At times we may step out of the narrative and take a more rational, objective view of ourselves, but it is usually the raw emotional power of these stories that drives our behavior. The breakthrough to axial thinking wasn't a turning point in human history because it displaced the earlier modes of thought, but because it proved incredibly powerful.

The power of myth and narrative is still deeply rooted in our psyche, but time and time again ends/means rationality has proven itself vastly superior at solving the problems we face. No matter how much psychological sense it makes to blame a grave illness on a malevolent supernatural source, if given the chance few of us would choose an exorcism over modern medical treatment. It's no exaggeration to say that the growth of axial thought has not only transformed the human world, but the planet as well. Whether or not that change will ultimately be for the good, however, is an open question.

As the authority of the mythic view of the world was undermined, so was its ability to shape our culture. That was, however, a slow process, measured in millennia, not years. None of the greatest figures of the Axial Age condemned the myths of their times or the gods who populated them; instead they observed a kind of polite distance. The propriety of the Confucian gentleman, for example, demanded that he carefully observe all the traditional rituals, not because he feared the wrath of the gods, but because to fail to do so would be offensive and inappropriate. The Buddha never denied the reality of the gods, but he didn't give them any particular importance either. The gods were bound by the same laws of karma as everyone else, and they were, at times, depicted as coming to the Buddha to seek his unsurpassed wisdom.

Even the spread of monotheism from the margins of civilization to its centers did not displace these mythic patterns of thought but merely narrowed their scope. The pantheons of gods and goddesses with all their conflicts and drama were supplanted by the single male God whose undisputed dominance was hardly the stuff of great storytelling. Local spirits and family cults survived for a time, but one by one most of them were snuffed out. Traditional soothsayers and magicians were condemned as servants of the devil, and the ecstatic celebrations of the past were banned.

Yet new myths and magics appeared to replace the old, the belief in angels and demons continued on, and new rituals and holy days were woven into the fabric of daily life. The vast richness of the old myths may have been lost, but the story of Jesus, the Son of God, and his miraculous power or of the boundless wisdom of the Prophet

Mohammad were told and retold in countless different ways. Priests and their elaborate rituals provided a direct avenue to salvation, and numerous cults sprang up around different saints who were thought to hold supernatural power to cure illness and bring fertility or material blessings.

As a religion without priests and with far less ritual, Islam generally took this process of disenchantment further than its Christian counterparts, although many strong mythic elements still remained in Islamic thought. Protestant Christianity, one of the latest arrivals on the monotheistic scene, and especially its Calvinist variants, were the most vehement opponents of the old worldview, for they evinced an open contempt for anything they saw as magical or superstitious. For the Calvinist, each of us is predestined to salvation or damnation from the time of our birth, and no religious rites, no amount of prayer or good works could make the slightest difference in our fate. As Weber put it is his classic treatise, *The Protestant Ethic and the Spirit of Capitalism*:

> The rationalization of the world, the elimination of magic as a means to salvation, the Catholics had not carried nearly so far as the Puritans. .... had done. To the Catholic the absolution of his Church was a compensation for his own imperfection. The priest was a magician who performed the miracle of transubstantiation, and who held the key to eternal life in his hand. One could turn to him in grief and penitence. He dispensed atonement, hope of grace, certainty of forgiveness, and thereby granted release from that tremendous tension to which the Calvinist was doomed by an inexorable fate, admitting of no mitigation. For him such friendly and human comforts did not exist.[6]

The question of why such a grim perspective as divine predestination gained purchase in Protestant theology is complex, but it certainly shows the way the rational systematic thought of the axial breakthrough came to permeate religious belief. The logic goes something like this: If, as most Christians believe, God is the supreme all-knowing and all-powerful creator of the universe, it follows that He knows the fate of every human before they are even born. Thus, each of us is predestined to salvation or damnation, and try as we might, nothing we do will alter our fate. Of course, other conclusions can be drawn from these same premises, but the brutal logic of predestination is obvious.

As radical as this and similar doctrines were, there is only so far the process of disenchantment can go within the confines of monotheistic belief. It remained for another scion of the axial breakthrough—the ideology of scientific materialism—to reject the beliefs in the salvation of heaven, the damnation of hell, and even God himself. The roots of scientific thought go far back into the ancient world, but what has been called the Scientific Revolution began in Western Europe in the sixteenth and seventeenth centuries—around the time John Calvin was formulating the Puritan doctrine. This new approach combined the rational systematic thought that characterized the axial breakthrough with a new effort to test its conclusions with experiment and empirical evidence. All the leaders of the Scientific Revolution were Christian believers, and at first the study of the natural world was encouraged as the study of the "wonders of God." But because the early scientists had to work within the confines of the Church's ideological hegemony, they often had to soften or conceal findings that conflicted with its theology. To a Hindu or a Taoist, it would seem puzzling that the belief the earth rotates around the sun might be a religious heresy, but Christian theology went far beyond the spiritual, and even as great a scientist as Galileo was found guilty of heresy, threatened with torture, and forced to recant the heliocentric model of the solar system.

As the amazing successes of the scientific approach piled one upon another, however, the balance of power shifted. In the nineteenth century, a number of influential scientists emerged from their laboratories and went on the offensive, pushing for the kind of intellectual and religious changes they felt were demanded by the knowledge scientists had discovered. They sold their beliefs to the public under the label of "science," but in so doing they overlayed something that was originally only a methodology with a self-confident new ideology. To them, of course, it was just common sense, and only religious views were unsubstantiated dogma. Alan Wallace's summary catches the essence of this new creed:

> According to these nineteenth-century crusaders, the message of science for human society is this: Existence is purely physical—there is no other reality. The sources of this reality are the laws of nature, forces that are entirely impersonal, having no connection whatsoever with the mind of human beings, their beliefs, or values. These laws operate in isolation from any supernatural, spiritual influences, all of which are illusory. Life in the universe is an accident, the outcome of mechanical interactions among complex patterns of matter and energy. The life of an individual, one's personal history, hopes and dreams, loves and hates, feeling, desires—everything—are the outcome of physical forces acting upon and within one's body. Death means the utter destruction of the individual and his or her consciousness, and this too is the destiny of all life in the universe—everything will eventually disappear without a trace. In short, human beings live encapsulated within a vast, alien world, a universe entirely indifferent to their longing, unaware of their triumphs, mute to their suffering.[7]

The dourness of this philosophy rivals that of their Calvinist opponents, to whom the scientific crusaders owed more than they realized. In this "scientific" perspective, damnation was replaced by total annihilation, but in both cases, we are completely powerless to do anything about it. In a sense, the Puritans were better off, since even though extinction might be preferable to eternal damnation, there was still a chance one might be among the small group of the elect that God has chosen to save (and most Puritans seemed to believe they were among its numbers). The new philosophy, on the other hand, held out no hope of escape to those terrified by the prospect of their annihilation.

While the Puritans were never more than a small percentage of the world's monotheists, this new "scientific" philosophy spread to the far corners of the globe. As countless cultures around the world were upended by the Industrial Revolution and the new scientific methodology gave birth to wonders only dreamed of in the past, this secular philosophy gained ever-growing status and prestige. Traditional religious beliefs and practices didn't just wither away in the face of this fierce new competitor, but they tended to retreat to a few special reserves. Various ceremonies and celebrations, avowals of faith by public figures, the occasional visit to a church on Sunday or a mosque on Friday, replaced the taken-for-granted acceptance of the religious worldview and left the everyday lives of many people disenchanted in a way they had never been before. In such a world, it's no wonder that Tara seems like nothing more than a strange fantasy.

Sources

The original idea that there was an "Axial Age" that transformed human civilization comes from Karl Jaspers, *The Origin and Goal of History* (London: Routledge and Kegan Paul, 1953). Robert Bellah's *Religion in Human Evolution: From the Paleolithic to the Axial Age* (Cambridge MA: Belknap/Harvard, 2011) is a more recent and very comprehensive treatment of this subject. Concerning the Axial Age in India, I was already quite familiar with the early development of Buddhism (see Coleman, *The Buddha's Dream of Liberation*; *Freedom, Emptiness, and Awakened Nature*, Somerville, MA: Wisdom, 2017), and Geoffrey Samuel's *The Origins of Yoga and Tantra: Indic Religions to the Thirteenth Century* (Cambridge: Cambridge University Press, 2008) helped fill in the broader Indian context.

Max Weber was once again an invaluable guide, and for this chapter I would recommend his most famous work, *The Protestant Ethic and the Spirit of Capitalism* (https://www.marxists.org/reference/archive/weber/protestant-ethic/). For an interesting examination of the origins of the ideology of scientific materialism, see Alan Wallace and Brian Hodel, *Embracing Mind: The Common Ground of Science & Spirituality* (Shambhala: Boston and London, 2008).

5

The Goddess Who Became a Buddha

At first glance, it's surprising that Tara ever made her way into the modern world, given the power of patriarchal religion and the global tide of secularization that were aligned against her, but the flow of history never goes in a single direction. There are always eddies, swirls, and countercurrents, and eventually the tide may turn. History shows us that the great feminine wisdom Tara embodies has broken through the walls of patriarchal rationalism time and time again, perhaps most tellingly in the wild Tantric ferment of medieval India where she found her current form. As a goddess, a Buddha, and an archetype of feminine spirituality, she seems uniquely suited to the needs of our times—for we face both a profound alienation from the natural world she embodies and what seems to be the oncoming crisis of the patriarchal ego.

Mythical Beginnings

Tara's name tells us a lot about who she is. Look in a dictionary of classical Sanskrit and it will tell you tara means "star" or "planet," and even today tara still refers to a star in modern Sanskrit-based languages. A more popular approach in Buddhism is to see Tara's name as a derivative of *tṛ*, the Sanskrit verb meaning "to cross" or "to traverse," but either way, the implication is the same. The ocean is a common image in Buddhism for the world of suffering, and whether Tara is the night star who guides us to the shore of liberation or the one who ferries us there, she is a liberator who helps free us from delusion and brings us to the awakened, transpersonal state.

Two common myths describe Tara's origins. One makes her seem more like a goddess and one more like an ordinary human being who realizes her inner buddha nature. The first one begins with the great Bodhisattva Avalokitesvara who is the very embodiment of compassion and the "One Who Hears the Cries of the World." As the story goes, one day he saw all the suffering of the world with an unflinching gaze—all the greed, hatred, and delusion, all the wars and injustice, the famines and the sickness. He was overcome by the thought that despite the countless number of beings he had brought to liberation, the number of suffering beings grew no smaller, and for this he wept. Tears streamed down his face and formed a pond, and from that pond a blue lotus holding the shimmering form of a beautiful woman appeared. She was a translucent green, her body was adorned with fine silks and jewels, and she quivered with the boundless energy of compassion. She was, of course, the great liberator Tara who promised to work tirelessly to help him to save all those trapped in misery and defilement. So in this story, she has the same kind of supernatural origins typical of the gods. Like Athena, she arose fully formed from the body of another deity, even if father Zeus's original motivation in eating his pregnant wife to prevent his offspring from challenging his power was, to say the least, less lofty than Avalokitesvara's.

In the other origin myth, Tara began as an ordinary woman, Princess Wisdom Moon, who spent lifetime after lifetime serving the Buddha of her era and perfecting her wisdom until she had a great opening in which she realized her own buddhahood. From that moment on, she dedicated herself to the benefit of all sentient beings throughout time and space. Along the way, she also issued a ringing challenge to the patriarchal attitudes so deeply rooted in India and Tibet:

> In the age called "Light of Various Worlds"
> There was a princess, Moon of Wisdom,
> Who devoted herself to the teachings of the Buddha, Sound of Drum,
> And for the first time she realized supreme bodhicitta (enlightenment).
>
> At that time, all the bhikshus (monks) exhorted her:
> "You should pray that you may be transformed into a man
> So that through the power of your merit,
> You can accomplish the full benefit of the teachings."
>
> The Princess Moon of Wisdom looked at the bhikshus and replied:
> "Here there are no men, there are no women,
> There is no self, no individual, and no perception.
> These labels as 'male' and 'female' are meaningless,
> The utter confusion of foolish worldly beings."
> Thus she taught the equality of all things.
> "Many are those," she continued, "who wish to attain enlightenment with a male body, but few who wish to do so with a female body.
> Therefore until samsara (the world of suffering) is emptied,
> I shall work for the benefit of all beings in the body of a woman."[1]

From the standpoint of her pure realization, Tara saw that all dualistic concepts—whether female and male, right and wrong, or samsara and nirvana—are only mental constructs and have no intrinsic reality. Though she didn't hesitate to use dualistic concepts when they were useful, the verse shows us that she had no tolerance for those who mistake such social conventions as gender for objective reality and use them for divisive ends.

The Historical Thread

Having explored India's great axial breakthrough and its leading figure, Siddhartha Gautama, let's pick up that thread and see where it leads. Over the following centuries, Siddhartha's followers grew from a small group gathered around a charismatic leader to a powerful, established religion that had a large network of monasteries and teaching centers. At the same time, his Brahmanical counterparts expanded their influence from North-Central India across the subcontinent, absorbing local cults and traditions, and spreading their system of ranked *varnas* which became the foundation of the Hindu caste system. Each caste was a part of a rigid hierarchy with its own rights, duties, and rituals, and despite their privilege, even the well-born had to follow a strict code of behavior and perform the right rituals to maintain their purity and avoid the dangers of "pollution."

In many ways, life was even more restrained for the Buddha's monastic followers. Despite Buddhism's doctrinal challenge to the reality of a self, the growing numbers of monks and nuns followed a disciple of what can only be described as extreme self-control. They had to wage such a constant war against their instinctual impulses for such things as sex, comfort, and more than one meal a day, that both Buddhists and Jains called those who had attained enlightenment "victors."

It will come as no surprise, then, that sometime around the middle of the first millennium CE, a religious uprising rose to challenge all those confining rules. Although it likely has even more ancient roots, one theory holds that the source of this movement was a low-caste group of "tantric" sorcerers who gained magical power from shocking violations of society's rules of purity and propriety. And shock they did, as we can see from this passage from one of the later tantric texts, the *Guhyasamaja Tantra*:

> Those who take life, who take pleasure in lying, who always covet the wealth of others, who enjoy making love, who purposely consume faeces *(sic)* and urine, these are worthy ones for the practice. The yogin who makes love to his mother, sister or daughter achieves enormous success in the supreme truth ...[2]

The quest for magical powers (*siddhis*) is a theme that runs through all the tantras, but as time went on and the movement expanded, the *tantrikas* became ever more concerned with higher spiritual goals and the pursuit of enlightenment. Their ranks came to include people from all walks of life—from kings and Brahmins to the lowest outcastes. Although they often carried out their practices in secret, there are many stories of *tantrikas* gathering in dark places associated with the burning of dead bodies and having ritual feasts where they would sing and dance, eat forbidden foods, drink wine, and have ritual sex. A whole range of new practices sprang up, and great tantric adepts, known as *mahasiddhas*, spread them far and wide.

The first Europeans to hear of the tantras were horrified, but Western attitudes toward the tantras are more positive today, even if the unsophisticated often think they are about nothing more than having great sex. Of course, some *tantrikas* were more interested in Dionysian revelry than anything else, but the tantric movement was far more than that. It added a host of new practices into India's already unparalleled arsenal of spiritual technologies and pioneered a radical new approach to the quest for liberation. As important as they were, the tantric sexual yogas were only a part of a more fundamental rethinking of the relationship between desire and the spiritual path. To the Buddhist monk or Hindu ascetic, desire is the snare that binds them to the suffering of *samsara.* To the *tantrika,* the fires of desire can also provide the power to bring them to liberation, if they can see through to the energy of enlightened wisdom at its core.

That may sound great in theory, but how can it really be done? The tantric texts that come down to us from that time give instructions for elaborate rituals with complex symbolism that often involve sexual union—real or imagined—but it is an open question as to how many of the *tantrikas* actually practiced them. Since most people of that age could not read or write, such texts must have been directed to a relatively small literate elite. A look at the legends and stories of the *mahasiddhas* from that period paints a fuller picture. The Tibetans have preserved a wonderful collection of stories of the lives and enlightenment of eighty-four of the great Indian masters from that period, and though many of them are too fantastic to be taken literally (one yogin, for example, lived in the belly of a great fish for twelve years), I find them to be a treasure trove of information about the tantric revolution.

At the heart of all these stories is a life-changing encounter between a student mired in confusion and a tantric teacher. None involve the study of any kind of text, and unlike today, the teachings were only given one on one, never in groups. There are only a couple of stories in which a student is given explicit instruction in the sexual yogas, but there are several more accounts of tantric couples who lived and practiced together for years at a time making their sexuality and their entire relationship a field for practice.

One of the most striking things in these stories is the vast array of practices they describe. Again and again, tantric masters tailor their instructions to the unique needs of each student. A musician is taught a meditation on sound. The Dharma is taught to a cobbler using the metaphor of shoemaking, and he is told to make his work his meditation. A compulsive liar is advised to contemplate all appearances as deceptive. Those puffed up with their lofty status are told they must violate the taboos of their caste by, for example, cleaning their teacher's toilet.

Of all the techniques pioneered by the Buddhist and Hindu *tantrikas*, the use of visualizations was probably the most groundbreaking. Visualization was only of minor importance in early Indian religion, but many of the Mahayana sutras paint elaborate pictures of the Buddha surrounded by retinues of followers and hosts of celestial beings. Monks were often instructed to visualize such images to call forth the Buddha's wisdom and support. The *tantrikas* progressively expanded these practices to deeper and deeper levels. Their most basic practices were similar to those of the Mahayana, except the object of meditation would often be a female who possessed frightening wrathful features. In more advanced practices, however, the practitioners would merge with their *yidam* (the enlightened being who was the object of their meditation), becoming one with her vast enlightened mind and whatever enlightened energy she symbolized.

The tantric movement was, in a sense, an uprising of the passion and spontaneity of the awakened feminine in a spiritual world dominated by masculine self-control. But what role did actual women play? The Indians were quite possibly the world's greatest philosophers, but their historical records are often sketchy, and the lack of solid evidence leaves us with a host of unproven theories. The founders of the tantras may well have been women whose stories were lost when male scholars and monks took over the movement and wrote them out of their histories. On the other hand, women and men may have participated as equal partners who worked selflessly to bring each other to enlightenment. Or the tantric movement may, like the rest of Indian society, have been dominated by men whose repressed sexuality was projected onto those frightening and powerful female images. In all probability, there is some truth in each of these ideas. Medieval India was an oppressive, patriarchal culture, but in the tantric world women seemed to have some measure of real authority. They were unlikely to have been scholars or intellectuals, since that world was largely closed to them. But there are countless stories of wise, powerful, and often frightening women who shattered the complacency of the spiritual seekers they encountered and opened them up to vast, unseen possibilities.

As is so often the case with such antinomian movements, the *tantrikas* slowly came to terms with the religious establishment, and their ideas and practices were absorbed into more orthodox Brahmanism and even into the Buddhist monasteries with their celibate monks. A body of tantric literature emerged that contained spells and elaborate rituals, while its most shocking and transgressive practices, such as the sexual yogas, came to be performed more in visualization than in the charnel grounds. Although powerful female figures, both historical and imagined, continued to play a central role in tantric practices, it was the men who ran the show.

While the tantric movement was developing its radical new approach to spiritual practice, feminine energy was erupting in popular Indian religion as well. Hosts of new, or at least newly popular, female deities who wielded awesome powers rose to prominence throughout the subcontinent. The central figure was Devi, the heir of the Great Goddess whose followers saw her as the supreme creator, sustainer, and destroyer of the universe. Durga, often considered a form of Devi, was a fierce warrior goddess who slayed a horrifying buffalo demon that none of the male gods could, and she is still among the most popular Hindu deities today. And then there are the *mahavidya* (great wisdom) goddesses we will encounter later in this chapter. Foremost among them is Kali, one of the most terrifying of all the Indian gods, often shown dancing on the body of her supine husband, Shiva, while holding a severed head dripping with blood.

Tara was, of course, a major part of this up-swelling of feminine energy. She may have originally been a Buddhist form of Durga. There is a passage in the Indian epic poem, the *Mahabharata*, referring to Durga as *Tarini*, "she who ferries across"—a phrase also applied to Tara—and at least forty-four of the names of Tara in the classic text, *The 108 Holy Names of Tara*, were also given to Durga. Over the centuries, however, Tara became completely distinct, manifesting more forms than any other Buddha or Bodhisattva in the Buddhist pantheon and winning enormous popularity among the common people.

Tara is often referred to as a "Mother Goddess" by Westerners, and there is no doubt that she was often seen that way in the patriarchal cultures of India and Tibet, where a woman's most prestigious and important role was that of a mother. But that is only one facet of her myriad appearances and characteristics. There are Green Taras, White Taras, Yellow Taras, Red Taras, and Blue/Black Taras which all represent different elemental energies. In some forms she has two arms, sometimes four, eight, or as many as a thousand. Sometimes she is radiantly beautiful, beaming with serenity and love. Sometimes she bares fierce fangs and powerful weapons. Sometimes Tara is sensuous and erotic, and sometimes horrifyingly frightful and ugly. But however she appears, she unfailingly manifests the enlightened energy of the awakened feminine, and the very diversity of her forms testifies to the protean nature of its power.

Even the *idea* of Tara being a fully enlightened Buddha was a reflection of the growing power of the feminine spirit. In earlier Buddhism, women were often seen as incapable of enlightenment, or rather that a woman first had to be reborn as a man before she could reach full awakening. The *Pali Canon*, which is among the earliest records of the Buddha's teachings, sends mixed messages. In one talk the Buddha is held to say that: "It is impossible, it cannot happen that a woman could be an Accomplished One, a Fully Enlightened One—there is no such possibility."[3] But in another sutta he says: "There are not only one hundred … or five hundred, but far more bhikkhunis (nuns), my disciples, who by realizing for themselves with direct knowledge here and now enter upon and abide in the deliverance of mind and deliverance by wisdom that are taintless with the destruction of the taints [in other words, they have reached enlightenment]."[4]

Whatever the Buddha's actual views, early Buddhism was highly patriarchal. The importance of women grew as time went by, however, and some Mahayana sutras explicitly declare the spiritual equality of women, while others still take the more traditional patriarchal view. By the time we get to the tantras, however, there is no doubt about the spiritual power of women. Not only did Tara herself condemn the misguided view that there is some kind of difference in the capabilities of women and men, but disrespect for women came to be considered a root downfall for the tantric practitioner.

In her early days, most of Tara's followers probably saw her as a powerful goddess who could help them with their daily problems. She was considered especially useful in vanquishing fears and anxieties. In the art found in the caves at Ajanta in what is now the Indian state of Maharashtra, we see how she gained power over the years. In its sixth-century art, it is Avalokitesvara, the male bodhisattva of compassion, alone who protects from the eight great fears and dangers. In one panel from the end of that century, he is accompanied by two goddesses one of whom is probably Tara, but by the seventh century Tara takes over from Avalokitesvara and saves beings from the eight great fears all by herself. All gods demand worship, and one of the earliest and most influential of the Tara Tantras, *The Twenty-One Praises of Tara,* extolls her boundless virtues, and even today it is often recited by her followers just as Christians might gather to "praise the lord." Many Tibetans know these twenty-one praises by heart and recite them in times of need or at joyful celebrations. They also tell countless stories of people who have called on Tara—by reciting her praises, repeating her mantra, or just calling out her name—who were saved from every kind of affliction from poverty to attacks by bandits or demons. She even has a form to help win the affections of one's object of romantic desire. For those few who had access to the sacred texts hidden away in the monasteries or a willing tantric teacher, Tara's power could also be invoked in magical rites and spells. The *Tara Tantra's Origin of All Rites,* like many other tantric texts, gives instructions for sorcery to gain such mundane things as good looks, affluence, long life, and strength, as well as for darker purposes such as subduing women and killing one's enemies. The use of Tara's power for such misguided purposes is obviously an affront to all the most fundamental principles of Buddhist ethics, and other parts of the same text, which was probably compiled from a variety of sources, admonishes devotes not to kill, lie, steal, or eat meat, and to honor women.

Despite her powers as a goddess, Tara was also considered a Buddha—a perfectly enlightened being—and there has always been a tension between Tara, the goddess who protects you from your fears and satisfies your desires, and Tara the Buddha whose enlightened presence inspires your selfless dedication to bring happiness, joy, and freedom to everyone. As time went on, the latter aspect of her nature became ever more important. For most of her followers, the main Tara practices were probably the recitation of her twenty-one praises, her 108 names, and descriptions of the ways she saves beings from the eight great fears. When she was made the object of visualization, she was usually external to the practitioners, either in front of them or above their heads. The practitioner might simply bask in Tara's presence while reciting her mantra or visualize purifying nectar or rays of light flowing from Tara into them. For the most advanced, meditations emerged in which the practitioner actually merged with Tara. In these, the practitioner sees their body as Tara's body. Not a body of flesh and blood, but a body of shimmering light endowed with all the enlightened characteristics of whichever Tara is the object of their practice. More importantly, the practitioner's mind merges inseparably with Tara's mind of enlightenment, and they become one with Tara's infinite love, wisdom, and power, and with her boundless desire to liberate all beings from their suffering.

Following the Muslim invasions of India in the twelfth century, Buddhism died out in its native land (it was reintroduced in the twentieth century, but that is another story), but Tara lived on. Although she was never as popular as the major Hindu gods, elements of her cult continued on in Hindu practice, particularly in her form as one of the ten *Mahavidya* goddesses. More importantly, she became a central figure in the Himalayan Buddhism to the North. Records of Tara's presence in Tibet can be found as far back as the seventh century, when the wife of a Tibetan king persuaded him to build a temple to house a statue of Tara she had brought with her from Nepal. It doesn't, however, seem that Tara was widely practiced until what is called the "second transmission" of Buddhism to Tibet in the eleventh century.

One of the key figures in this movement was the great Atisa, an Indian scholar and yogi who was a fervent devotee of Tara. According to legend, it was Tara herself who persuaded him to move to Tibet in his later years to help spread the Dharma. Atisa was not allowed to translate the Tara Tantras because Tibetan orthodoxy held them to be too great a risk to public morality, but he did translate several White Tara texts which were based on the personal revelations of the Indian mahasiddhi Vagisvarakirti, and he taught Tara practice directly from his own personal experience.

The classic tantras that provided the scriptural authority for Tara practice slowly worked their way into Tibet over the next century, and as the restrictions on tantric practice dissolved Tara became a central figure in all the Tibetan lineages. One Tibetan text holds that: "all the disciples of Atisa and of the Conqueror Tsongk'apa [founder of the Gelug sect of Tibetan Buddhism] took Tara as their highest deity, and prayed to her alone; especially the Omniscient Gedundrub [the first Dalai Lama] would do whatever he did only after he had prayed to the holy Tara."[5] The Sakya sect felt that Kurukulla, a passionate red Tara with four arms, was the special protector of their lineage, and the Kagyu sect is especially connected with White Tara. Of course, the monks and lamas have a vast array of buddhas, bodhisattvas, and *yidams* in addition to Tara, but there is no question that Tara and her male counterpart, Avalokitesvara (Chenrezig in Tibetan), are the center of the devotion for the common people of Tibet. As strange as it sounds, Tara even came to be identified with an ogress, "lustful and lascivious and full of desire," who was considered one of the mothers of the Tibetan people.

Isolated in their towering mountains, the Tibetans were among the most inward-looking people in the world until the twentieth century, but the diaspora that followed the Chinese invasion of Tibet in the 1950s changed all that. Pockets of Tibetan Buddhism spread around the world, and Tara came with them. From there, she gained a foothold among practitioners of other Buddhist traditions as well as in many forms of New Age spirituality. Nonetheless, she still faces two daunting obstacles in the contemporary world. In ancient times, the cult of various deities could easily spread from land to land, and no one thought much about it. The monotheistic religions that still dominate much of the world's religious landscape, however, often put up fierce resistance to any challenge to their hegemony. Tara is either dismissed as primitive superstition or condemned as an affront to the one true male God. On the other hand, while the rational systematic approach of the Buddha's early teachings have had considerable appeal among secular materialists, Tara seems to embody all the elements of traditional religion that they reject. Yet the tides of change are running in Tara's favor. In the West, patriarchal Christianity is in decline, and while the incredible accomplishments of science have fed a tidal wave of secularization throughout the world, it has left many people adrift and searching for a spiritual foundation. And at the same time, the shift from agriculture to industrialism and the flood of women into the labor force has opened vast new horizons for women and kindled a palpable longing for the feminine wisdom that has been repressed for so long. As a fully enlightened *female* Buddha, at least to me, Tara embodies both the wisdom of the awakened feminine and its raw power in a way no other figure can.

The Awakened Feminine

In the Hindu tradition, *shakti,* the primal cosmic energy that makes life possible, is female. The fiery power of *shakti* blazes in all life and without it the universe would be empty and inert. The symbolic representation of this power is, as we have seen, Mahadevi (also known as Devi) and her followers not only consider her the supreme godhead of the universe, but that all the other goddesses are aspects of her. Foremost among them are ten strange and exotic Hindu tantric goddesses called the *Mahavidya* (great wisdom) goddesses who at first glance are certainly puzzling. David Kinsley, one of the leading scholars of the Indian goddess traditions, had that same reaction:

> What is one to make of a group of goddesses that includes a goddess who cuts her own head off, another who prefers to be offered polluted items by devotees who themselves are in a state of pollution, one who sits on a corpse while pulling the tongue of a demon, another who has sex astride a male consort who is lying on a cremation pyre, another whose couch has as its legs four great male gods of the Hindu pantheon, another who prefers to be worshiped in a cremation ground with offerings of semen, and yet another who is a hag like widow?[6]

It's hard to imagine a more diverse group than these ten, but they have much in common. First, they all seem to revel in the transgressive and the unclean—anything and everything that orthodox Hinduism says to avoid. Second, in contrast to the strict patriarchy of orthodox Hinduism, they are never shown in the role of a submissive wife (although some are said to be married to Shiva), and when they do appear with a male god they are always in a position of dominance. Third, unlike the luminous beauty of so many goddesses we have encountered, the *Mahavidyas* often appear in terrifying forms. But perhaps most important, the cults of all the tantric goddesses involve more than just prayers, offerings, and sacrifices at their temples and shrines. Their highest form of worship involves inner practices that allow the adept direct access to their powers (*siddhis*) and even spiritual liberation itself.

Foremost among the Mahavidyas is the terrifying Kali. Although the various lists of these goddesses vary in order and sometimes even in length, Kali is always first. She is clothed only in a skirt made of severed arms and a necklace of human heads, and she holds a sword and the severed head of a man that is dripping blood. Her face shows

Figure 5.1 *Goddess Kali with severed head dancing on Shiva. Artwork by Raja Ravi Varma (1848–1906), retouched reproduction by Aavindraa. Public Domain.*

pure fury, and gleaming blood trickles from the corners of her mouth. Her eyes are bulging and her tongue lolling out grotesquely, suggesting insatiable lust. She is the sexual aggressor, sometimes shown having sex astride her male consort who is lying on a funeral pyre. More often, she is standing atop the supine body of her husband, Shiva, who seems powerless before her fury. Her hair is wild and unbound, her companions are ghosts, jackals, and furies, and at her temples she is pleased by blood sacrifice (see Figure 5.1).

Though not nearly as popular as Kali among Hindus, Tara does have her place and is always second on the list of the ten *Mahavidyas*. Of all the other *Mahavidyas*, she is the most like Kali, sometimes considered her emanation or junior partner. Consider this description from a medieval Hindu text:

> Tara should be conceived as emerging from a white lotus. She advances with her left foot forward, and she is dreadful in appearance. She is short in stature and has a protruding and long belly. She wears a garland of skulls and a tiger skin skirt. She is

> eternally young. Her forehead is decorated with a row of five skulls. She has a lolling tongue, she is very dreadful and has four arms in which she carries a sword, a pair of scissors, a cut head, and a lotus ... She has three eyes; she stands on a blazing funeral pyre; her teeth are dreadful; she is adorned with ornaments.[7]

Like Kali, Mahavidya Tara is usually dark blue/black and is commonly shown sitting or standing on a male corpse or on the reclining body of Shiva. Their most striking differences are Tara's big belly and protruding breasts which suggests that she has a stronger connection to nurturing and fertility, and indeed, Mahavidya Tara does have her peaceful compassionate forms. Like her Buddhist counterpart, she is a savior who helps ferry people across the raging torrents of *samsara* to safety on the other shore.

There are still a number of active Hindu Tara temples scattered across Northern India and Nepal—the most famous of which is Tarapith in rural Bengal. Worship in this temple tends to emphasize Tara's maternal aspects. In its central image, she is depicted nursing a young Shiva, and she holds court in the temple routinely dispensing favors to her devotees like an understanding mother. Yet she has her fierce aspects. A three-foot-tall metal statue in the temple depicts her savage form, and next to the temple is a cremation ground in which yogis perform traditional meditations that sometimes involve corpses. The most striking contrast with Buddhist Tara, though, are the sacrifices. Mahavidya Tara is sometimes described as "she who likes blood," and two or three goats are sacrificed to her every day in the temple and hundreds more on special ritual occasions.

I won't explore all the other Mahavidya goddesses here, but I can't move on without mentioning one of the most striking and perplexing of all—Chinnamasta. She is blazing red and usually depicted standing or sitting on the bodies of a couple locked in a sexual embrace (although sometimes she herself is having sex with a man lying beneath her). The most shocking thing about this image is that she is holding a sword in one hand and *her own freshly severed head* in the other. Blood squirts from her neck in three streams—one feeds her own head and the others feed two naked female companions who are holding swords of their own. This strange and powerful image is subject to countless interpretations, but it appears that by cutting off her head with all its thoughts and conceptual elaborations, she is able to channel the primal life force (*shakti*) generated from copulation to feed and sustain herself and her companions.

Before we explore the Buddha Tara's many forms and functions, we need to look at the other mysterious manifestation of the awakened feminine in the Buddhist tradition—the *dakini*. As we've seen, Buddhism was originally a very masculine affair, and there was little in the way of female imagery or symbolism. The original dakinis were considered repulsive figures—witches and horrifying ghouls who ate flesh and reveled in the suffering they caused. But as Buddhism began to open to the feminine, a new kind of *dakini* rose to prominence. Like Tara, the *wisdom dakini* is a beneficial figure who seeks only to help people on the spiritual path. In one sense, any woman can be said to be a *dakini*, since everyone contains the seed of awakening, but for our purposes at least, such a definition is both too broad and too narrow. Too broad because many women never realize their wisdom potential, and too narrow because the ranks of *dakinis* also contain ethereal beings far beyond the human. Literally, *dakini* means something like "sky dancer"—a wonderful metaphor for the complete freedom of her enlightened mind.

The legends of the great tantric siddhas are full of stories of their encounters with the *dakini* in dreams and visions, and in the flesh. She may appear as a powerful supernatural presence or as something quite mundane, like the yogi's consort or his mother. Whatever her form, the *dakini* serves to shock the yogi out of his complacency and self-centered delusion and guide him to the true spiritual path. The story of Naropa, the great scholar and tantric practitioner who was one of the founders of the Kagyu school of Tibetan Buddhism, is a classic example. Naropa was a brilliant intellectual who had great confidence, if not arrogance, about his understanding of the Dharma; and he rose to be the abbot of Nalanda, the great Buddhist university in India. One day, the story goes, he was out walking, and met a shriveled old hag who demanded he tell her if he understood the words of the Buddha's teachings. When he told her that he headed the great university and that, yes, he knew the words of the Buddha, she seemed quite happy, but then he added that he understood their meaning as well. At that point the woman fell into a frenzy, crying and pulling her hair. She screamed that although he was a great scholar, Naropa was also a liar, and that if he was ever to find the true meaning of the Dharma he had to study with her brother, Tilopa. Naropa realized at once that this was no ordinary woman, but a great wisdom *dakini*, and he vowed to follow her instructions. He left the university on a long quest that led him to Tilopa, and ultimately to his own liberation.

Despite their surpassing wisdom, or perhaps because of it, the *dakinis* are mysterious figures. There are many stories of an individual who encounters a *dakini* but fails to recognize her, and thus loses the priceless gift of the wisdom she offers. The stories that come down to us of these encounters are mainly about men, but of course the *dakinis* appear to women as well. As Judith Simmer-Brown points out in her insightful book, *Dakini's Warm Breath,* the *dakini* often plays a different role for the yogini than for the yogin. She appears to both at key points in their spiritual journeys, but while she often shocks the yogin out of his complacency and arrogance, she is more likely to welcome the yogini as her sister and point out her true *dakini* nature.

The *dakinis* play another vital role in Tibetan Buddhism as well. Like Tara, they are the objects of advanced visualization practices, which is to say they are used as a *yidam. Yidams* come in many shapes and forms. They can be a buddha, a bodhisattva or a *dakini*; female or male; glowing with peaceful beauty or the most terrifying vision imaginable. Whatever their form, they allow practitioners to work with the primal energies of their minds in ways other meditation practices cannot. The *dakini* most often called into service as a *yidam* is the great Vajrayogini—the blazing red "diamond yogini." She is what's called a "semi-wrathful" figure. Unlike wrathful *yidams*, she isn't hideous or terrifying. She is extremely beautiful, yet not a symbol of tranquility, for she radiates a raw, threatening sexual energy. In most images, she stands completely naked, bares frightening fangs, drinks blood from a cup that's made of a human skull, and wears a necklace of severed human heads. Some texts say that she is an emanation of Tara, and it can be difficult to distinguish her from many of the forms of Red Tara. Vajrayogini does not, however, come in the bewildering array of forms that Tara does. She is more of a specialist, yet she is nonetheless a pure manifestation of the awakened feminine whose essence is indistinguishable from Tara's.

What exactly is Tara's essence? Many of her devotees worship her and ask for help with their daily problems in the way they might with any other goddess. Green Tara grants protection from fear and danger, White Tara bestows longevity, Red Tara helps in winning the object of one's romantic desire and subduing enemies, Yellow Tara brings prosperity and abundance, and in all her forms Tara is seen as a savior—the "swift one" who responds immediately to any call for help. Yet Tara is also a Buddha which is entirely different. A goddess is a mighty being who, as Campbell suggests, represents the overpowering natural forces that confront us as an external reality. A Buddha, on the other hand, lies within—a manifestation of our deepest true nature.

Becoming a Buddha is *to realize what we already are* or, at least, to realize the hidden potential buried within us.

If we compare the Buddha Tara with the great goddesses of human myth, it is her differences that stand out. As we've seen, Tara has several origin stories, but almost all the myths and legends about her say that she comes to the aid of those in need. She saves people from fires, plagues, famines, and wars, and restores lost wealth and vitality, but there's nothing about her having any kind of personal life. She is never depicted with a husband or children. There are no accounts of her getting into fights with other gods as we see in so many other mythologies. She never journeyed to the underworld, and she doesn't seem to have played a role in the creation of the universe.

Perhaps most interesting, she doesn't seem to have an individualized personality in the usual sense. Inanna was powerful and impulsive, Isis loving and nurturing, Aphrodite sunny, cheerful, and full of erotic passion, while Athena was rational and calculating. Although Tara manifests all the great human emotions, she does so in their purest form, untainted by even a hint of selfishness or personal concern. She is the very embodiment of love and compassion, yet her love is so universal and unbounded that she doesn't show the slightest preference for one being over another. The vast power of her anger is truly terrifying, but she only wields it to destroy the bonds that cause us to suffer, never for petty personal ends. She is sometimes shown in a sexual embrace with a consort, but their passion is a pure manifestation of the energy of the awakened mind and is never bound by personal romantic attachment. In contrast, many gods are depicted as proud, jealous, or arrogant, demanding worship and obedience even to their most unreasonable commands. They show favoritism to their children and those they love, and a callous disregard toward those they don't. Those who defy them are likely as not to suffer a grizzly fate.

To be a Buddha like Tara is wholly different. She transcends all personal needs and prejudices and dwells in the boundless equanimity that sees the true nature of reality behind all individual expression. She fascinates because she puts us in touch with facets of our deepest true nature that lie hidden beneath the swirling confusion of our minds. She appears in a feminine form because that is most useful in this time and place, but she is not in any way bound by the dualisms of male and female. Given the protean nature of the awakened feminine, it is hardly surprising that Tara comes in more forms than any other buddha, bodhisattva, dakini, or yidam.

Reciting the "Twenty-One Praises of Tara" is one of the most popular devotional practices among her followers. In the influential school of interpretation founded by the Indian siddha Surya Gupta, a layman she miraculously cured of leprosy, each praise is directed to a distinctly different form of Tara. These Taras are green, white, yellow, red, and blue/black. Some have two arms, some four, some as many as twelve. Many are peaceful and serene, others display a terrifying wrath, while still others are somewhere between. She usually has two or three eyes, but she can have as many as nine, and in a few forms she even has three faces. Her different forms hold a variety of symbolic objects such as a flailing knife, a bow and arrow, and a lotus flower, and she holds her hands in various *mudras* (gestures) that symbolize, for example, generosity, wrath, or protection. Yet even these twenty-one forms are far from a complete list of all her countless manifestations.

All this may be bewildering to those new to her tradition, but this boundless diversity provides an important clue to understand what Tara is really about. As a fully enlightened buddha and the essence of the awakened feminine, Tara doesn't have any real physical form. All her forms, like everything in this world of *samsara*, are no more substantial than a rainbow or a mirage. She manifests them out of compassion to provide people a way to see into their own nature and thus free themselves from the delusions that are causing their suffering. Every manifestation of Tara arises in response to the needs of a particular individual or situation, and she appears in whatever form will be most beneficial. So, while she has many traditional forms and is depicted in many traditional ways, she is in no way bound by them. In spite of all the paintings, statues, and carefully worded descriptions, it is doubtful that any two people ever envision her in exactly the same way, yet the power of the awakened feminine shines unfailingly through all her genuine manifestations.

Some versions of Tara are more well-known than others, and it helps to know which forms she most often takes. You might think that the color a *thangka* painter chooses for Tara's skin is merely a matter of aesthetics, but it actually is of the upmost symbolic importance, and it is the best guide to her myriad forms. That is why she is called White Tara, Green Tara, Red Tara and so forth, even though she has countless different forms in each of these colors. The symbolic meaning of each color is based on the belief found in many ancient cultures that the world is made up of five elemental forces—earth, fire, water, wind, and space (or air)—and that each one is associated with a different color.

In the Surya Gupta system, Green Tara is the one from whom all other Taras arise, and she is the one most often depicted in paintings and sculptures. Although she is usually shown in her peaceful form, there is a wonderful seventeenth-century Thangka from the Rubin Collection that shows Green Tara in her "semi-wrathful" form with fangs, a tiara of skulls, a necklace of human heads, and eight different arms each holding a different ritual instrument. She is surrounded by Black, Red, Yellow, and White Taras reflecting the full spectrum of her power. Green is associated with the wind element, and it is Green Tara who performs all the various kinds of enlightened activities. She pacifies those who are agitated, nourishes those in need of support, magnetizes people to come together for their mutual betterment, and destroys what blocks the path to realization.

Each of the colors is associated with a defiling emotion that must be transformed, and for green it is jealousy. The most common form of Green Tara shows her with a very human body—two arms, two eyes, and two legs—albeit one of surpassing beauty and grace. She is sitting in "the heroine pose," with her left leg bent and right leg extended so she can instantly jump to the aid of any being who needs her help. Her right hand is held downward with her palm facing forward in the mudra of generosity. In some practices, meditators imagine that nectar is flowing from her right hand into their body, cleansing them of defilements and filling them with divine love. Tara's left hand is held upright with her third finger touching her thumb—the mudra of protection—and she holds the stem of a lotus flower blossoming next to her left ear. The lotus grows in mud and its exquisite blossom is a symbol of the possibility of transforming suffering into the wisdom of enlightenment. She is arrayed in the finest silks and jewels, and her radiant smile is both peaceful and mysterious.

White Tara is also extremely popular, perhaps because she is believed to bring health and longevity. White is the color of space and is associated with the vast open awareness of the enlightened mind. Its defiling emotion is the confusion and doubt that arises from ignorance of our true nature. In what is perhaps her most common form, White Tara sits in the lotus posture that is so popular for meditation (cross-legged, with the left foot placed on the right thigh, and the right food on the left thigh)—a reflection of her unshakable repose in enlightened awareness. In this form, she has two arms, one face, but seven eyes—three in her head and one in each of her hands and feet. These are called the eyes of "wisdom awareness," and they allow her to gaze compassionately on all the suffering of the world. She has a loving smile, and like Green Tara her right hand opens in the mudra of generosity and her left in the mudra of protection. Her color is often likened to the luminous glow of the moon, and she radiates the brilliant colors of the rainbow in all directions. None of the White Taras in the Surya Gupta practice have exactly these attributes, but they are all surpassingly beautiful, and they all shine with love and compassion. One of the most vivid is White Moonlight Tara, who stands erect with twelve arms and three faces—a white face in front, a blue one on the right, and a yellow one to the left. Although she isn't in a classic meditation pose, her first two hands are in the mudra of meditative equipoise and the others bear a staff, a treasure vase, and a holy text.

Green and White Tara are the object of popular devotion throughout Tibet and the Himalayas, and countless laypeople call upon them for protection and long life. Red Tara and her comrade Vajrayogini are more the subject of esoteric visualization practices than popular cults. Red represents the fire element, and Red Tara is often visualized standing in the midst of blazing flames. Red is also associated with desire, passion, and lust, and Tara's four-armed form as Kurukulla and the two-armed form of Vajrayogini are often shown standing naked upon a human corpse and blazing with eros. They have frightening fangs and wear a necklace of human heads dripping blood. Vajrayogini is frequently shown locked in a fiery sexual embrace with Chakrasamvara or some other male *yidam*. She stands on one leg with her other leg wrapped around her lover with a ferocious expression on her face. The five Red Taras in the Surya Gupta practice, on the other hand, tend to emphasize her power more than her sexuality. Her forms are described as heroic and victorious, and are said to dispel suffering, subdue hindrances, and destroy attachment.

Yellow is the color of the earth element. It represents abundance and prosperity, and its defiling emotion is pride. Yellow Tara is not as common in popular worship or esoteric practice as those other three Taras, yet in the Twenty-One Taras practice, a yellow/golden/orange Tara appears more often than any other. Perhaps most typical is Tara number twelve: She Who Grants Prosperity and Auspicious Circumstances. Her body is yellow or golden. She sits in the lotus position and has eight arms. Her right hands hold a trident, a hook, a vajra (representing a diamond that cuts through delusions), and the sword of wisdom. Her left hands hold a jewel next to her heart, a hook, a staff, and a "prosperity vase" (or a pot of money). Tara number twenty, Tara Source of All Attainments, is orange or coppery golden in color. She has only two hands and holds a single wish-fulfilling vase at her heart which cures illness and grants all attainments.

Dark blue/black is the color of water.[8] Surprisingly for most Westerners, water is associated with the force that holds things together and with the afflictive emotion of anger. Most of the other Taras are divinely beautiful even when displaying their wrath, but not the dark blue/black Taras. Tara number fourteen, Wrathful Shaking and Frowning Tara, is, for example, truly horrifying. Her body is black, and her wrathful faces are black, red, and white. Each face has three red eyes staring angrily, and all three faces are frowning with brows and lips contracted while devouring a plate of human entrails. Each head is wearing a tiara of skulls, and each face is described as having "wrathful wrinkles." Wrathful Shaking and Frowning Tara stands on a human corpse while wearing a necklace of severed heads. She has six arms, and in her hands she holds a sword, a hook, a staff, a cup made from a human skull dripping with blood, a noose, and Brahma's head. (The *yidams* of tantric Buddhism are often shown with symbols depicting their superiority to the Hindu gods.) She wears colorful snakes as ornaments and stands in the midst of blazing flames. It is hard to imagine anything more different from the peaceful beauty of the Green and White Taras, but she only uses the terrifying power of her rage for the same ends as the peaceful Taras—the liberation of all beings from their suffering. She fiercely smites the earth with the palm of her hand, pounds it with her feet, and emits a thunderstorm of vajras that destroys all the demons and harmful beings in the seven levels of the world.

***

If we look back over all the various forms Tara takes and all her myths and symbols, it is hard not to marvel at the incredible abundance of the human imagination. Many would dismiss them as mere fantasies, but real or not, they embody the most profound wisdom of the human experience. The fact that we try to repress and ignore her message makes it all the more urgent. It's understandable if the very abundance of her symbols and forms is confusing and perhaps a bit overpowering as well, yet if we look closely enough, we discover the protean diversity of the awakened feminine that underlies them all.

Sources

The Tantras are a tricky subject, but Geoffrey Samuel's *The Origins of Yoga and Tantra: Indic Religions to the Thirteenth Century* (Cambridge: Cambridge University Press, 2008) was once again vital in providing a clear exposition of its social and cultural background. Keith Dowman's *Masters of Mahamudra: Songs and Histories of the Eighty-Four Buddhist Siddhas* (Albany: State University of New York, 1985) provides invaluable translations and commentaries that help us see to the heart of the tantric revolution. For an argument that the founders of the tantric movement were female, see Miranda Shaw, *Passionate Enlightenment: Women in Tantric Buddhism* (Princeton, NJ: Princeton University Press, 1994). If you have some background in Buddhist philosophy and want to delve into an original tantric text,

I would recommend David Snellgrove's *The Hevajra Tantra: A Critical Study* (Oxford: Oxford University Press, 1980).

One of the best historical sources on the Tara cult in English are Martin Willson's translations of original Tara texts and commentaries from Sanskrit and Tibetan, *In Praise of Tara: Songs to the Saviouress* (London: Wisdom Press, 1986). Susan A. Landesman's *The Tara Tantra, Part I: The Root Tantra* offers a translation of the root text of the Tara Tantra as well as some detailed academic commentary. Stephan Beyer's *Magic & Ritual in Tibet: The Cult of Tara*, gives a detailed description of the Tara practices of Tibetan monastics, and is also one the best sources on the history of Tara practice in Tibet. The great late sixteenth-and early seventeenth-century Tibetan scholar, Jo Nang Taranatha, has a book, *The Origin of Tara Tantra* (Dharamsala, India: Library of Tibetan Works and Archives, 1995), but it is more concerned with mythology than history. The introduction in Kenpo Karthar Rinpoche's *Wish-Filling Wheel: The Practice of White Tara* (Kingston, NY: Rinchen Publications, 2009) traces the historical lineage of White Tara Practice in Tibet; and a good summary of what we know about the general historical origins of Tara practice is Dharmachari Purna's "Tara: Her Origins and Development," *The Western Buddhist Review*, Vol. 2 (1997). Rachael Stevens's *Red Tara: The Female Buddha of Power and Magnetism* (Boulder, CO: Snow Lion, 2022) is the definitive work on Red Tara and contains another excellent overview of what we know of Tara's origins.

6

The Transformation of the Psyche

Joseph Campbell once wrote, "In most mythologies, whether primal or from the high civilizations, deities are personifications of the energies of nature. The energies are primary, while the deities are secondary."[1] It follows that we need to know far more about Tara than her history and the cult that grew up around her practice. The key is to understand the nature of the primal energy she embodies, and how it resonates in our hearts and minds. Since Tara is a female Buddha, we can say almost by definition that she is a manifestation of divine feminine energy—what the Hindus call *shakti*, the power that makes all life possible. The key question here is how has that primal energy shaped the evolution of consciousness in our individual psyches and in our species?

Unfortunately, the guides who led us through Tara's history are not the ones to lead us here. The evolution of the psyche leaves only vague hints subject to conflicting interpretations in the archaeological record, the research of ethnographers, and the volumes of history. To learn more, we must look within, and here we enter an ambiguous realm that challenges the imperatives of the rational mind.

The greatest resources I found in this quest are in the riches of the world's myths and symbols, yet by their very nature, our great symbols are nested in layers of meaning that shift illusively as we try to pin them down. So what follows is one interpretation of many—a myth about our myths that tries to make sense of the transformation of our species' consciousness. Perhaps it is best judged by the resonance it holds for you, rather than a rational assessment of its truth or falsity.

As we begin our journey into the depths of the psyche, we need a new guide, and one of the best is the analytic psychology of Carl Jung and his followers. Most Western psychologies never took our myths, symbols, and dreams very seriously, but the Jungians place them at the center of their understanding of the psyche, and they've done more than anyone else to explore their depths.

Within the vast symbolic array of human culture, the Jungians discern a few basic "archetypes" such as the "mother," the "senex" (wise old man), and the "trickster." Inspired by a long tradition going back to Plato, the Jungians see these archetypes as basic structures that shape the psyche, and they are the foundation of what he called the "collective unconscious." As its name implies, Jung and his followers feel that it is shared by all humanity, prefigures and directs all our conscious behavior, and manifests its own unseen dynamics as well. Most Jungians use their understanding of symbols and myths in psychotherapy, but some have turned it to the exploration of the evolution of human consciousness. Foremost among them is Jung's student Erich Neumann, and it is his work we will depend on most heavily. Jung himself said that Neumann's "conclusions and insights ... are among the most important ever to be reached in the field."[2]

For all its insight, Jungian psychology has its limits for its practitioners often make the same error Joseph Campbell found among the followers of the theistic traditions—they mistake the symbol for the mysterious ungraspable reality to which it points. To become Tara is not to become an archetypal symbol, but to realize our deepest true nature. Symbols are a gateway—both a way the mysterious, primordial energy of our psychic depths manifests in our conscious mind, and a passageway into those depths. So as we explore the riches of the Jungian tradition, it is important to remember that our mythic symbols are representations that stand for something else, not independent entities in themselves.

Campbell was sympathetic to the Jungian approach, but he avoided many of its distortions, and I found his work to be a trustworthy guide to comparative cross-cultural mythology. For the development of the psyche, I depended on Neumann's penetrating understanding as well as the work of Ken Wilber. Although Wilber is less fluent in mythological thought than Neumann was, he has a unique insight into what we might call the philosophy of consciousness and the overall evolution of human spirituality.

With all that said, it would be hard to have much confidence in any understanding of our psychic evolution based entirely on the mysteries of our myths and symbols. We need to build our interpretations on some kind of more easily verifiable skeleton, and I found it in a surprising place—the process of psychological development each of us undergoes as we grow from infancy into adulthood which fortunately has been carefully studied by modern developmental psychology. As we will see, there is a direct parallel between the psychic development that occurs in each individual and the general evolution of consciousness in society as a whole.

The Evolution of Consciousness

If we go back to the earliest humans, or perhaps even further to our prehuman ancestors, there must have been a point at which we had little conscious awareness of any separation between ourselves and our natural environment. Like most animals, we responded to challenges from instinct and learning, without a conceptual understanding of what it means to be a separate individual or, for that matter, without conceptual understanding of anything else.

Whether it came slowly or in one dramatic leap, the development of self-conscious awareness was certainly the most fundamental turning point in the history of our species. When we first came to recognize our individuality, we still saw ourselves as an inseparable part of the natural world, totally dependent upon it and the social groups to which we belonged. As language developed ever greater complexity, a new layer that we might call mythological thought was overlaid above our earlier patterns of consciousness, but the dominant myths and symbols of those times still reflected our sense of dependence on the power of the natural world. Great mother goddesses symbolized the overwhelming importance of nature and the fertility of the earth, and there were magical forms of the animals we depended on for our food that took on human characteristics and exercised great power.

As time went on, our growing technological skills slowly transformed our relationship to the natural world. We moved away from our original habitats and into the built world of the towns and villages, and transformed the countryside into plots of agricultural land devoted to the cultivation of a few favored plants. Our dependent relational sense of self slowly gave way to what might be called the "heroic ego," and with it came the growth of logical, systematic thought—what we called the axial breakthrough in Chapter 4. Mythologically, this transition gave birth to the first stories of the great heroes who struggled to break free of mother nature and win their autonomy and dominion.

All this may sound like mere speculation about what is admittedly a bygone era, but we can see this same pattern playing out again and again in each individual's journey from conception to adulthood. We all begin in the womb in mute unity with our mother. Only after the trauma of birth and the early months of infancy pass, do we begin to gain some understanding of ourselves as an individual being separate from her and the power of nature she embodies. But the mother figure (which in some cases can be a biological male) is still of overwhelming importance—we are totally dependent on her just as early humans were totally dependent on the natural world.

Our journey through the later stages of childhood to adolescence and adulthood centers around the quest to establish an independent sense of ego and autonomy, just as our ancient ancestors struggled to break away and establish their independence from the vagaries of the natural world. We slowly learn that we are not only separate from our mother, but that we have an independent agency apart from hers. As we age, this sense of self becomes stronger and stronger until it literally comes to dominate our psyche. Virtually every action and experience is evaluated in terms of personal self-interest, and we begin an endless monologue of "self-talk," reveling in our successes, ruing our failures, and spinning out a never-ending story of who and what we are.

This developmental process is marked by profound changes in the way we think. As a child enters the vast symbolic world of language, she begins with what is often called "magical thinking." A doll has a human form, therefore it is a living being and is given a name and a personality. A toy spider is dangerous because it looks like a real spider. The child can protect herself from impending danger by closing her eyes to blot it out. But although these habits of magical thinking are never far beneath the surface, a more rational systematic mode of thought becomes ever more important as we age and must confront the demands of an impersonal world; as it did when our species moved from traditional to industrial society.

Although this may make it sound as if the evolution of consciousness comes in orderly stages in which we pass from one to the next until we reach the highest level, our development actually comes more in small increments than big jumps, and the earlier levels of consciousness persist no matter how strong a superstructure is built upon them. The primal terrors of the mythic realm lie just beneath even the strongest ego's quest for rational self-control—just as ancient myths and symbols live on in our postindustrial world.

Rather than as clearly defined stages, I think of the transformation of the psyche in terms of three great but admittedly ambiguous and evasive symbols—the Goddess, the Hero, and the Buddha. It is understandable that those accustomed to the clarity of empirical reasoning are uncomfortable with the uncertainty built into this kind of mythological understanding. But it is the shifting, multidimensional nature of such thinking that guards us from reification or oversimplification, and it can even provide tantalizing hints about the direction the future may take that a more rationalistic analysis inevitably misses.

Our personal and our social journeys both start from the dark "pre-personal" world of unreflective unity, and it is from here that the first flickers of conceptual understanding lead us to the discovery of both our separation and our dependence upon family, community, and the natural world—that is to say we discover the Goddess. As time goes on, heroes with their individualism and self-concern challenge the Goddess and struggle to subject her to the demands of the ego. Of course, the primal instinctual energy of the Goddess can never really be subdued, any more than we can deny the incredible transformative power wielded by the radical self-control and systematic thought of the hero. Sometimes the hero and the Goddess struggle in self-destructive conflict, sometimes they come to a working compromise, or control may ricochet back and forth between them, but whatever their dynamics, there are endless variations with great forward leaps and regressive falls.

Eventually, the glimmerings of a synthesis that incorporates the wisdom of the Goddess and the strength of the hero may start to emerge. The classic images of a male Buddha sitting in the cross-legged lotus posture gives us a feeling for what this synthesis might be like. He seems to rest in complete peace and equanimity, embodying a deep wisdom far beyond psychic conflict. Yet at least to me, he also appears withdrawn and aloof from the chaos of this world of suffering, and it is hard to see how he could represent a path forward for the struggling masses of humanity. If, however, we look at the images of Tara or some other female Buddha, we get a very different feeling. She shows the same transcendental peace, but at the same time she appears intimately connected to the life of the world. In many images, she has a radiant, loving smile and a glowing warmth, while her right leg is extended forward so she can leap to the aid of anyone who is suffering. She is passionately involved in the world, but at the same time rooted in a transcendental wisdom that brings her beyond egocentric attachments and concerns. Yet while Tara appears as a female, remember that her form is nothing more than a symbolic manifestation of the great transcendent wisdom that lies beyond all dualism. As Tara herself told us over a thousand years ago: "Here there are no men, there are no women, There is no self, no individual, and no perception. Labels such as 'male' and 'female' are meaningless. The utter confusion of foolish worldly beings."[3]

The Eternal Circle

What was it like to live in the primordial Eden of our ancient ancestors without conceptual thought or understanding? What is the undifferentiated awareness of the fetus in her womb? Our rational, egoic mind can only take our understanding so far, for concepts cannot tell us what it was like to live without concepts. The mysterious wisdom of our great symbols is a far better guide. When we look at them, we seem to have an immediate intuition of what they mean, yet that understanding somehow lies just beyond our grasp. Try as we might, we cannot seem to put it all into words, and when we try, it is our poetry not our prose that speaks most loudly.

One such symbol is the eternal sphere—self-contained, beyond time or space, without beginning or end. This is the primordial state in which all opposites are united, the eternal state without female or male, or if you prefer with them with both united. This is the germ from which all things arise. Plato himself, that pillar of the Axial Age, recognized the perfection of the Eternal Sphere. In the dialogue of Tiamaeus, which many believed to be the culmination of the author's intellectual achievement, Plato says:

> the demiurge [a cosmic being he also called the craftsman] made the world in the shape of a sphere, giving it that figure which of all is the most perfect and most equal to itself... And he established the universe, a sphere revolving in a circle, one and solitary, yet by reason of its excellence able to bear itself company, and need no other friendship or acquaintance.[4]

A closely aligned symbol is that of the circle—perfectly round and complete. Even more evocative is the uroboros, a snake that forms itself into a circle by eating its own tail—a symbol that Neumann discovered everywhere from the ancient Babylonians, Phoenicians, and Egyptians to the Navajo Indians and European Romani (see Figure 6.1). Of course, the snake appears as a mainstay of mythological thought in one form or another across the world, and even in places where they are unknown, substitutes are often found. The Polynesians, for example, have myths of a great eel who plays the role the snake would hold in other parts of the world. But the snake that is devouring its own tail has a very special meaning. In Neumann's words:

> It slays, weds and impregnates itself. It is man and woman, begetting and conceiving, devouring and giving birth, active and passive, above and below, at once .... This round and this existence in the round, existence in the uroboros, is the symbolic self-representation of the dawn state, showing the infancy both of mankind and of the child.[5]

Even though there is no separation of the female from the male in the uroboric state, it is often described with the metaphor of the mother. Lao-tzu, the greatest sage of China's Axial Age, put it this way:

> There was something formless yet complete,
> That existed before heaven and earth;
> Without sound, without substance,
> Dependent on nothing, unchanging,
> All pervading, unfailing.
> One may think of it as the mother of all things under heaven.[6]

Figure 6.1 *Uroboros drawing from a late medieval Byzantine Greek alchemical manuscript.*

It's easy to look back on this primordial state with all the confusion and ambivalence of our modern minds and see it as a kind of blissful paradise—no problems, no choices to be made, no unsatisfied needs, and totally at one with the universe. That is certainly how Freud, Jung, and Neumann all looked at it. In Neumann's words, being in the uroboros is: "lying inert in the unconscious, merely being there in the inexhaustible twilit world, all needs effortlessly supplied by the great nourisher—such is that early beatific state ... it gives nourishment and pleasure, protects and warms, comforts and forgives. It is the refuge for all suffering, the goal of all desire."[7] Campbell says much the same thing: "The state of the child in the womb is one of bliss, actionless bliss, and this state may be compared to the beatitude visualized for paradise."[8]

This attitude is reflected in the Hebrew mythology that was inherited by both the Christians and Muslims. The biblical metaphor for the uroboric state is, of course, the Garden of Eden—that paradisiacal place where Adam and Eve lived in unreflective happiness. The fall from paradise began when Eve ate from the fruit of the tree of the knowledge of good and evil—an act that had been forbidden by God—and then persuaded her husband to follow suit, in other words, when they started thinking in dualistic terms. In the usual understanding of this story, however, the root of original sin is not so much dualistic thinking, as woman's failure to obey the commands of the patriarchal father/God.

It is even possible to read the descriptions of nirvana in Buddhism's most ancient texts as a description of the uroboric state. In one passage, the Buddha rejects everyday reality with all its cravings as "unfit for delight," and then goes on to say:

> The escape from that is calm, permanent,
> a sphere beyond conjecture,

unborn, unproduced,
the sorrowless, stainless state,
the cessation of stressful qualities,
stilling-of-fabrications, bliss.[9]

Yet despite how commonly uroboric unity is seen as a kind of deep mystical state, I think that's a mistake, conflating the transcendence of ego with a state in which the ego has simply not yet developed. As Ken Wilber put it, some "imagine that Eden was some sort of transpersonal heaven, whereas it was simply a pre-personal slumber. This archaic-uroboric period does indeed appear angelic in many ways, but it is the bliss of ignorance, not of transcendence."[10] The sense of uroboric unity is not ultimate unity, but a unity based on ignorance—a singularity that has never known division.

The uroboros is not selfless—far from it. It is totally self-absorbed, self-concerned, and self-centered. It is unitary only because it recognizes no other. It is not what is termed in Sanskrit as *jñana*—timeless awareness or primordial wisdom. Rather it is a kind of the *vijñana*—divided awareness—that makes up our everyday consciousness. We like to think that the gazelle wandering the ancient savanna was completely at one with the natural world, but her world never extended beyond her immediate sensory field. Everything else was so completely other that it was entirely ignored. Of course, the uroboros does not represent fully developed self-consciousness, but it is the germ from which that consciousness develops, and as such, it already has the roots of separation and division within it. Buddhists call it the *alaya vijñana*—the "store consciousness" that holds all the seeds that ultimately manifest in our lives and is the foundation of all future psychic development.

The Separation

From this uroboric unity, opposites arose—light and dark, female and male, heaven and earth, subject and object, passive and active, self and other. The ying/yang symbol—the eternal circle half filled with black, and half with white, each trailing off into the other—is their classic expression (see Figure 6.2). The dark supports the light, and the light supports the dark, and both are contained within a single circle. Neither opposite can exist without the other, and, indeed, they both exist *within* each other. That is why the ying/yang symbol is often drawn with a circle of light within the darkness and a circle of darkness within the light.

It's easy to trace the fall from Eden and its uroboric bliss to the emergence of an original sense of separation. The world was divided, and we came to see ourselves as separate from one another and our environment. The first primitive sense of self arose, and within that construct, we saw our fragility, our dependence, and the inevitability of our death. Such was the price for the ability to think, for conceptual

Figure 6.2 *Yin and Yang.*

thought is simply impossible unless we divide the world up into discrete categories our minds can grasp.

How did this original division, this fall from Eden, arise? It seems that all the world's people have some kind of creation myth. On the surface, these myths are about the creation of the world, but when we look more deeply, we see that for most of the world's peoples, the genesis of human consciousness was the beginning of the world, and these myths apply just well to that momentous event as to the creation of the physical universe.

Of all creation myths, those of the Chinese stand out most vividly, for they do not see the original separation as the result of the intervention of someone or something from outside. In most traditions, it's a god or another powerful being who separates earth from sky, mother from father, and female from male. The problem with that is, of course, if some god or powerful being stands apart from the uroboric oneness, division and separation has already taken place, so such a being cannot be its ultimate source.

A wonderful verse at the beginning of Chapter 42 of Lao-tzu's *Tao Te Ching* gives the essence of the Chinese perspective:

> Tao produced the One.
> The One produced the two.
> The two produced the three.
> And the three produced the ten thousand things.
> The ten thousand things carry the yin and embrace the yang, and through blending of the material force(*ch'i)* they produce harmony.[11]

The *Daoyuan (Origins of Tao),* a Chinese text from the fourth century BCE, says it this way:

> Of old, in the time before there was Heaven and Earth: There were only images and no forms. All was obscure and dark, vague and

> unclear, shapeless and formless, and no one knows its gateway. There were two spirits, born in murkiness, one that established Heaven and the other that constructed Earth. So vast! No one knows where they ultimately end. So broad! No one knows where they finally stop. Thereupon they differentiated into the yin and the yang and separated into the eight cardinal directions. The firm and the yielding formed each other; the myriad things thereupon took shape.[12]

Most other creation myths symbolize those cosmic forces as great gods, but one basic theme occurs again and again: The world begins with the original state of uroboric unity, followed by the separation of opposites—usually the female earth from the male sky—followed by their sexual union and the proliferation of beings.

The oldest creation myths we know come from ancient Sumer, and they reflect the same primacy of the feminine we see in the psychic development of the infant. The sea is often associated with the primal unity of the uroboric state, and it was Nammu, the goddess of the sea, who alone existed in the beginning. She was the mother who gave birth to the heavens in the form of An, the sky father, and the earth in the form of Ki, the earth mother. After fierce Semitic invaders swept up from the deserts to the south and conquered the Sumerians, this myth was recast. The world was subjugated to male authority, and the great female creator was destroyed. In the *Enuma Elish*, the Babylonian creation myth, Nammu is renamed Tiamut, and this time the story begins with her resting in uroboric unity with her male partner, Apsu.

> When on high the heaven had not been named
> Firm ground below had not been called by name,
> Naught but primordial Apsu, their begetter,
> (And) Mummu-Tiamat, she who bore them all,
> Their waters commingling as a single body[13]

Tiamut and Apsu produce many gods as children, but those gods become so unruly that Apsu decides to destroy them, and when he fails, he is murdered by the god Ea and his supporters. Tiamut is enraged, and she creates a horde of monsters led by her new consort to destroy the offenders. Her opponents choose Ea's son, Marduk, as their champion, and after a fierce battle he slays Tiamut, cleaves her head open with an axe, and creates the heavens and earth from her body. From that time on, he reigns as king of the gods.

This fascinating tale lends itself to countless interpretations. The most obvious is the subjugation of the Goddess to the patriarchal gods of the invading pastoralists, but there is deep psychological meaning as well. As Neumann points out, whether or not a particular individual is female or male, her subconscious with its deep instinctual roots is usually symbolized as female, while her ego is usually symbolized as male. So, the conquest of Tiamut is the conquest of the instinctive uroboros by the rational ego, and her division into the primal opposites of heaven and earth represents the dualistic thinking which is the predominant mode of the egoic process. As long as Tiamut remains whole, the ego can never escape her instinctive power.

Despite being separated from Mesopotamia by more than 100 generations and nearly 10,000 miles, the creation myth of the Maori of Aotearoa (New Zealand) is remarkably similar:

> Rangi and Papa, the heaven and the earth, were regarded as the source from which all things, gods, and men originated. There was darkness, for these two still clung together, not yet having been rent apart, and the children begotten by them were ever thinking what the difference between darkness and light might be. They knew that the beings had multiplied and increased, and yet light had never broken upon them, but ever darkness continued ....

At last worn out with the oppression of darkness, the beings begotten by Rangi (the father) and Papa (the mother) consulted among themselves, saying "let us determine what we shall do with Rangi and Papa; whether it would be better to slay them, or to rend them apart." Then spoke Tu-matauenga, the fiercest of the sons of Tangi and Papa, "It is well; let us slay them."

Then spoke Tane-mahuta, the father of forests and of all things inhabiting the forests, or that are constructed of trees, "Nay, not so. It is better to rend them apart, and then let Rangi stand far above us, and Papa to lie beneath our feet. Let Rangi become as a stranger to us, but the earth remain close to us as a nursing mother …."

Their plans having been agreed to, Tonogo-ma-Tane, the god and father of cultivated food, arose that he might rend Rangi and Papa, he struggled but he did not rend them apart. Next Tangaroa, the god and fish and reptiles arose …, Next Haumai-tikitiki, the god and father of food that springs without cultivation arose …., Tumatauenga, the god and father of fierce human beings, arose and struggled, (but they all) struggled ineffectually.

Then at last, Tane-mahuta, the god and father of forests, of birds, and of insects, arose and struggled with the parents; in vain with hands and arms he strove to rend them apart. He paused; firmly he planted his head on his mother Papa, the earth, and his feet he raised up against his father Rangi, the sky; he strained his back and his limbs in a mighty effort. Now were rent apart Rangi and Papa, and with reproaches and groans of woe they cried aloud: "Wherefore do you thus slay your parents? Why commit so dark a crime as to slay, to rend us, your parents apart?" But Tane-mahuta paused not, he regarded not their cries and their groans; far, far beneath him he pressed down Papa, the earth; far, far above him he thrust up Rangi, the sky. Hence the saying of old time: "It was the fiercest thrusting of Tane which tore the heaven from the earth,

> so that they were rent apart, and darkness was made manifest, and light made manifest also."[14]

In addition to the obvious similarities to its ancient Mesopotamian predecessors, this later myth adds important new elements. The victims are crying out and condemning their attackers for the foul crime of murdering their parents. The guilt of this act is the same guilt that stems from the "original sin" in the Genesis tale. Through the heroic act of dividing the opposites, the ego steps forth from the magic circle of the uroboros and finds itself lonely, afraid, and feeling guilty about what it has done. The more independent the ego becomes, the more aware it is of its vulnerability and the terrifying shadow of the death that awaits it. The ego strives to repress all those feelings and the guilt that goes with them, but it is never entirely successful. They inevitably reappear in symbols, dreams, and inexplicable fears and confusions.

This creation myth, like so many others, pivots around "light." The children of Rangi and Papa were "were ever thinking what the difference between darkness and light might be," and were "worn out with the oppression of darkness." Light illuminates the world and is therefore a symbol of conscious awareness as opposed to the darkness of the uroboric unconscious. Knowledge is born in the light of rational awareness, but that act of cognition cleaves the world into opposites; for it is only through dualistic conceptualizations that the world is known, and with that knowing come fear, isolation, and death—the inevitable companions of the power that knowledge brings.

The Goddess

At this stage of development, we often see the emergence of two central gods, a female and a male, but they are never equal. The female always rules. This inequality is clearest when we look at the individual human psyche. As we've seen, original separation is often represented by cosmic opposites—dark vs light, earth vs sky, ying vs yang—but the original separation in the human psyche is "self" vs. "other" or, more accurately, "self" vs. "mother." As Louise Kaplan put it, the "mother is the one partner with whom the baby plays out the separation drama."[15] The father or other male figures are of little importance. Even when a biological male is the primary caregiver against whom the infant struggles to separate herself, he is still enacting the archetypal role of the Great Mother.

When the dim realization that she is separate from her mother first dawns in a child, she feels an ever-growing sense of fear and anxiety. She is so small and weak compared to the Great Mother; so totally dependent on the mother's care and protection. Her mother's slightest displeasure is terrifying for if the mother merely neglects to feed her, she will soon starve. At this stage of development, the mother is of such overwhelming importance that the image of the Great Mother dominates the child's psyche. Two forms of the Great Mother appear over and over in the mythologies of the world: the peaceful "good mother," who provides nurturance, support, and care, and the "wrathful mother," who withholds her love and threatens pain and destruction.

In the original uroboric state, there are no symbols. But as the psyche becomes differentiated enough to recognize the distinction between mother and self, the biological mother becomes the Great Mother, the one who holds the power to grant or deny the child's most basic needs. The good mother allows her child to retreat into uroboric bliss as she suckles at her breast or cuddles against her warm body, but she also allows her to return to the world of individual awareness when she is satisfied. The wrathful mother, on the other hand, leads her children back into the silent unity of her womb, destroying every trace of their individuality—an annihilation from which only she can grant return.

Although the picture is less clear, there is evidence of the cultural primacy of the feminine among our most ancient ancestors as they were first emerging into self-awareness. As we have seen, the remains of humankind's first cave paintings and figurines reflect both the male world of the hunt and the female world of family and reproduction. However, in the great cave paintings human males played a relatively minor part in comparison to the animals of the hunt, while almost all the figurines that have been found are of more or less human females with large breasts and full figures reflecting the awe with which early humans held women's power of fertility. It seems likely those carvings depict the Great Goddess as a "powerful being" on whom the human community depended for its prosperity and survival.

If we fast-forward through history, the vast number of female figurines found in remains of the goddess cultures of Old Europe leaves no doubt that the Great Goddess rested at the core of those ancient civilizations. As humankind moved from foraging and simple farming to more complex hierarchical societies, the Great Goddess took on the characteristics of a queen who as was said of the great Sumerian goddess Inanna, "ruled over heaven and earth."

The Great Goddess embodies the natural world with her primal power over, birth, death, and everything between. Campbell describes the multivalence of the goddess symbol this way:

> On the simplest level, then, the Goddess is the Earth. On the next, archaic, level she is the surrounding sky. On the philosophical level, she is Maya, the forms of sensibility, the limitations of the senses that enclose us so that all our thinking takes place within Her bounds—she is *IT.*

This ancient statue from Minoan Crete shows the Great Goddess in all her primal glory (see Figure 6.3). Her fierce expression and protruding breasts give witness to her boundless power, which is also symbolized by the lioness on her head and her furious stare. The snake often accompanies the Great Goddess as it did Eve in the Garden of Eden. In this image, she holds a snake in each hand, symbolizing her connection to the primal forces of nature and her iron grip on the male power of the phallus.

Both psychologically and culturally, the good mother and the wrathful goddess are inseparable parts of a single complex. But as

Figure 6.3 *A Cretan snake goddess from the Minoan civilization, c. 1600 BCE. Credit: C messier, Wikimedia Commons, CC BY-SA 4.0 License.*

human cultures turned in an ever more patriarchal direction, the wrathful goddess was split off from the good mother, and slowly driven from conscious awareness into the lower depths of the psyche. The Virgin Mary, mother of God, is a classic example. She is among the few archetypal symbols of the Great Goddess who survived the hegemony of patriarchal monotheism, but we see only her "good" side. She is always kind, loving, open, and caring. The wrathful power of the feminine is split off and denied, for the Virgin can never be angry or vengeful like the all-powerful male God. Mary is not only a classic symbol of the good mother because she's nurturing and compassionate, but also because she is completely asexual. She even had a baby without ever engaging in the carnal act. She is entirely devoid of the Great Goddess's ferocious erotic passion that is so threatening to the power of the heroic male ego.

In pre-Christian myths, the good mother had a sexual side, but as the power of the patriarchy grew, it was directed exclusively to her husband, who she nurtured and protected as she did her children. Isis, for example, was the loving wife of the god Osiris, and as we have seen, she was an archetype of the good mother throughout Egypt and later in the vast expanse of the Roman Empire. In her myths and in the minds of her countless devotees, she was never threatening or wrathful, always ready with loving support in times of need. Sita played much the same role in India. Despite what by contemporary standards seems like abuse and neglect from her husband, Rama, she remained ever-loyal and submissive to his will.

There is an obvious connection between the wonders of childbirth and reproduction and the fecundity of the natural world. In countless cultures around the world, people called upon some form of the Great Goddess when they wanted to conceive a child or guarantee the fertility of their fields. But though the gift of fertility shows her benevolence and compassion, it is inevitably wedded to her fearsome wrath. Sometimes she becomes angry and withholds her bounty. The crops don't grow, and famine stalks the land,

Yet even when the wheat or the corn grows high, eventually it dies and decays, and becomes fertilizer for the soil—reminding us of the unavoidable fact that where there is birth, there is death. Decay, disruption, and death are the inescapable price for new life to arise—a price that must sometimes be paid in blood. Whether it is the bleeding of her monthly cycles, of sexual initiation, or of childbirth—the female is always associated with blood. So it is not surprising that in many cultures the Great Goddess demands blood to fertilize the land and make it bloom. Originally, the sacrificial blood was often human, but even when the victim was a goat, a lamb, or a bull, as became more common in later times, the principle remains the same. Although male gods sometimes required blood sacrifice as well, far more often it was the Goddess who demanded blood.

Another reason the wrathful side of the Great Goddess was so prominent in the ancient myths is that she embodies the forces of the natural world which so often overpower the human struggle for autonomy. On a psychological level, the ego is haunted from its very inception by the dread of dissolution and a return back to the maternal womb. Again and again, the myths show the wrath of the Great Goddess who crushes the attempts of the fledgling ego to separate from her.

The ego is always represented by the male in these stories, and although the reason he offends the Great Goddess varies, as do the ways he meets his fate, at this stage the outcome is always the same—his death. In one version of the myth of Hippolythus that was recounted by the great Greek playwright Euripides, he was a hunter and sportsman who was disgusted by sex and marriage. As a result, he only worshiped Artemis, the virgin huntress, and refused to honor Aphrodite. Enraged at his disrespect, she cursed Hippolythus by causing his stepmother, Phaedra, to fall madly in love with him. When he discovered her love, he was revolted, and he roughly rejected her and her advances. Humiliated, she killed herself but left a note that accused Hippolythus of raping her. When Hippolythus's father read the note, he was infuriated, and he prevailed upon the great god Poseidon to send a sea monster to destroy his son while he was off on his hunt. The monster frightened Hippolythus's horses, who bolted and threw him out of his chariot. He became entangled in the chariot's reins and was dragged to his death. Poor Actaeon, on the other hand, merely had the misfortune to come upon the goddess Artemis (known to the Romans as Diana) while she was bathing in the nude. Amazed by her ravishing beauty, he stopped and stared, and as punishment for his disrespect, she turned him into a deer, and he was promptly torn to pieces by his own dogs.

Those who fall victim to the Great Mother's lust often suffer a different fate. Attis was abandoned by his mother when only a child, but he grew into a long-haired beauty, and Cybele, the great mother of the gods, fell in love with him. To protect him, his parents sent him away to marry the daughter of a king, but Cybele appeared at the wedding displaying all her radiant beauty and power. It was too much for any mortal. Attis was struck with madness and in a symbolic denial of male power, he castrated himself and soon died. Cybele later repented and saw to it that Attis's body should neither rot nor decay, and Attis came to be a god of fertility, who like the fruits of the land, dies in the winter only to rise again in the spring. The Phoenician story of Eshmun is much the same. He was a beautiful young man who loved hunting and fell victim to the lust of Astarte, who was a goddess of the hunt along with war, sexuality, and healing. She pursued him so ferociously that he fell into helpless despair, and like Attis castrated himself and died. Astarte took pity on him, returned him to life with the warmth of her own body, and made him a god of healing.

The Hero

As the power of the ego grows, the hero (the symbolic embodiment of ego) struggles to resist the fatal seduction of the Great Mother. Knowing that only death and dissolution await her lovers, the hero finds a way to resist and survive. The oldest recorded legend of the hero's journey, the *Epic of Gilgamesh*, drives the point home. After Gilgamesh and his faithful companion Enkidu, return from slaying the fearful demigod, Humbaba, and stealing the trees from the forest Humbaba defended, the great goddess Ishtar attempts to possess him—as the wrathful goddess always does in one way or another. When the Princess Ishtar [a later form of Inanna] saw Gilgamesh dressed in his finest clothes and wearing a crown, she was so struck by his beauty that she asked him to marry her and become her lover. She promises him a chariot of lapis lazuli and gold, a house with the fragrance of cedar, a grand throne, and that kings and princes will bow down to him. But Gilgamesh stands his ground, and tells her:

> Which lover didst thou love forever?
> Which of thy shepherds pleased [thee for all time]?
> Come, and I will [name for thee] thy lovers;

Gilgamesh recites a long list of the men Ishtar has loved and then destroyed, and then concludes:

> If thou shouldst love me, thou wouldst [treat me] like them.[16]

Ishtar is enraged at his affront and looses the ferocious Bull of Heaven to destroy Gilgamesh and his city. The bull kills hundreds of young men until Gilgamesh and Enkidu cut it to pieces in a fierce battle.

When Ishtar curses Gilgamesh for his deeds, he and Enkidu throw the hind quarters of the bull in her face.

This classic story makes another telling point about the heroic ego: Where there is ego and separation, there is the fear of death. After their victory, the gods debate how to punish the two men for their deeds, and they decide that Enkidu must die. Once his beloved companion is gone, Gilgamesh goes into mourning and is seized by an overwhelming fear of his own death.

> Enkidu, whom I love deeply, who went through every hardship with me, the fate of mankind has overtaken him.
>
> Six days and seven nights I mourned over him and would not allow him to be buried until a maggot fell out of his nose. I was terrified by his appearance!
>
> How can I stay silent, how can I be still! My friend whom I love has turned to clay. Am I not like him? Will I lie down, never to get up again?[17]

Gilgamesh decides to take a long and perilous journey to the underworld to secure the secret of immortality. After many trials, he nearly succeeds, but in the end his hopes are dashed and he must accept the destiny the gods have decreed for all men.

The vast array of Greek myths and stories that survived into the modern era offer a host of depictions of the hero's journey, but none are more famous and enduring than *The Odyssey*, first written down more than a thousand years after the *Epic of Gilgamesh*. It is a far longer and more complex tale full of great drama and high adventure that has much to tell us about the evolution of the heroic ego.

In contrast to the *Epic of Gilgamesh*, the Great Mother/wife plays a central role in this mythic tale. In the *Iliad*, the other great poem attributed to Homer, Odysseus (known as Ulysses to the Romans),

King of Ithaca, is forced to leave his beloved wife, Penelope, and his infant son to go abroad to fight in the Trojan Wars. Even after decades of absence and uncertainty, Penelope is ever faithful to her husband, ever kind and gentle, and ever submissive to the appropriate male authority whether it be that of Odysseus or of her son after he grows into a man.

After ten years of war, it takes Odysseus another decade of trials and tribulations to finally make his way home to Penelope. Throughout his great odyssey, he is guided by the goddess Athena. Although she shows him all the love and support of a bountiful mother with none of the seductive dangers the wrathful goddesses so often bring, he has to confront that raw power in other forms, including seductive nymphs and female monsters that block his way.

Odysseus's tale of return starts as he sets sail for home, with a fleet of ships. The winds blow him to the city of Ismarus, which he and his men quickly sack. He urges them to flee with the loot, but lacking his heroic self-control, they refuse. Just as Odysseus feared, they're met with a vicious counterattack that forces them to run to their ships in disarray. After a fierce storm, they make shore in the land of the Lotus-eaters. When his crew eat the "honey-sweet fruit," they fall into a peaceful lethargy wishing nothing more than to stay there with the Lotus-eaters forever. Odysseus is confronted with the ego's greatest fear–dissolution into the passive seductions of the unconscious—and he is forced to drag his men, one by one, back to their ships and to the world of rational self-control.

After setting sail again, they land on the island of a frightening cyclops and another of giant cannibals, from which they barely escape with their lives. Finally, they arrive on the island of a beautiful nymph known as Circe. When his men first approach her house, they find her singing in a spellbinding voice and weaving a divine cloth of enchanting beauty. She invites the enthralled men to dine with her—then feeds them a potion that turns them into pigs. Once again Odysseus's crew has surrendered their rational self-control, and once again Odysseus saves them—this time with the help of the great god Hermes, who gives Odysseus a potion to protect him from Circe's magic. When Odysseus drinks Circe's magic brew and remains unfazed, she is amazed. She quickly realizes who he is and tries to lure him to her bed, but before he consents to be her lover, Odysseus demands she swear an oath never to plot against him again.

From then on, she is his ally, and when she sees him grieving at the loss of his friends, she agrees to free them from her spell. Odysseus spends the next year resting in her enchanting company, but his men eventually grow restless, and she agrees to help them make their way home. But before they can set sail for Ithaka, Circe tells Odysseus they must go to the Kingdom of the Dead and consult the ghost of the great blind seer Tiresias. When Odysseus finds him, he makes many dire predictions, but he also gives him this advice: "Even so, you and your crew may still reach home, suffering all the way, if you only have the power to curb their wild desire and curb your own, what's more."[18] As always, rational self-control is the key to the survival of the egoic hero.

After they return to Circe's island, she provisions them with supplies and warns of the dangers that lie ahead. In such tales, the ocean represents the depths of the instinctive mind, and they must sail past three great dangers that threaten watery doom. First, there are the sirens—seductive females whose thrilling song lures sailors to their destruction on the rocks. Following Circe's sage advice, Odysseus plugs his men's ears with beeswax, so they cannot hear the sirens' call, but he has himself lashed to his ship's mast so he can listen to the unbearable sweetness of their calls to death ringing in his ears.

Once safely through, they must sail between two hideous female monsters. Scylla rises up from her sea cavern and devours all who come too close with her six heads and terrible fangs. Deadly Charybdis, on the other hand, gulps entire ships down her watery maw. Six of Odysseus's men are snatched up in Scylla's mighty jaws and die, but Odysseus and his remaining crew sail through to safety on the island of Helios, the sun god. After all seems saved, Odysseus's crew once again fall victims to their lack of self-control, and eat the sun god's forbidden cattle. They are immediately beset by evil omens, and as they sail away the mighty Zeus smashes their ship to pieces, and only Odysseus survives. Clinging to his mast, he is washed up on the island of another lovely nymph, Calypso, with whom he stays for seven years as both her captive and her lover. Finally, Athena persuades the gods to set him free, and Odysseus makes his final journey home, triumphant. His ego has withstood the seductions and the terrors of the primal depths, and stands victorious as an exemplar to all who follow this new path of psychic development.

Neumann tells us that as patriarchal society strengthens its cultural grip, the fierce and wrathful aspects of the Great Goddess are split off and driven into the unconscious, and only the good mother/wife remains in view. That certainly is the case in the *Ramayana*—the most famous and beloved of all the epic tales of the hero's journey. The central story of the *Ramayana* is strikingly similar to that of the *Iliad*—the wife of a powerful ruler is kidnapped and held captive by a rival king, and her husband launches a long and bloody war, defeats his enemies, and brings her back home. The husband in this case is Rama, a form the great god Shiva takes on when he decides to be born a human, and his mate is Sita who embodies all the characteristics of the good mother/wife. Even after she is kidnaped and held captive by Ravana, king of the demons, Sita spurns his endless advances and remains ever loyal to Rama. While Rama has to face countless difficulties in the struggle to save his wife, he never encounters the seductive nymphs or the monsters from the unconscious depths that tried to block Odysseus's way. So, it seems this tale is a product of a later stage of psychic development. The power of the wrathful goddess that threatened Odysseus has been entirely banished, and the central female image is the loving mother and faithful wife who offers nothing but support and encouragement to the male ego.

As these heroic myths evolved over the centuries, the stories changed but the central themes remained. Set to writing almost two millennia after *The Odyssey*, the classic Old English tale *Beowulf* added some elements of the code of chivalry that was beginning to emerge in Northern Europe, but like all the classic heroes, Beowulf seeks to prove his egoic manhood in the face of extreme adversity. When he faces the monster Grendel, who had driven Beowulf's ally Hrothgar from the Mead Hall where he would drink and celebrate with his men, Beowulf decides that since Grendel has no sword, fairness demands that he confront him unarmed as well. After a furious battle, he kills the beast and later slays his mother when she comes to avenge Grendel's death. When their adventures are over, the men drink and celebrate, and sing the praises of Beowulf's manly virtue. In many stories of this kind, such as *St. George and the Dragon*, the hero saves a princess or a maiden from a beast, but in *Beowulf* the women only serve the men their mead and bolster up their egos. All that counts is the great heroes' fame and the glory of their deeds.

Yet after the hero banishes the wrathful goddess and leaves only the good mother in her stead, what then? What are the essential characteristics of this patriarchal hero? Throughout all his trials, it's his strength, bravery, and determination that set him apart from lesser men. He tries things that no other man would try and achieves things no other man could achieve. His conquest of the feminine, whether he was challenged by her seduction or her fury, leaves him powerful and in control. He is no longer a part of the herd, but something truly special. In addition to his battle-tested strength, the egoic hero has a calm calculating mind and a steely self-control over the turmoil of his uroboric depths, and he rules over others with the same kingly power as he rules himself.

In the centuries since these tales were first told, we have added layer upon layer to their mythic core, and today's heroes may seem a very different breed. Instead of a kingly lord of the established order, our hero is more likely to be an outsider seeking justice in a corrupt world—defending the weak and bringing down the mighty. It is his unbending sense of fairness that sets him apart from other men, something we see foreshadowed in the Beowulf's heroic tale. Today's hero often lives alone or wanders free from social bonds, using his strength to set right society's wrongs—or at least to struggle in heroic futility to achieve his noble goals. Consider Bellah's description of the myth of the "hard-boiled detective":

> [The] detective must be tough, and above all, he must be a loner. He lives outside the normal bourgeois pattern of career and family. As his investigations begin to lead him beyond the initial crime to the glamorous and powerful center of the society, its leaders make attempts to buy off the detective, to corrupt him with money, power, or sex. This counterpoint to the gradual unraveling of the crime is the battle the detective wages for his own integrity, in the end rejecting the money of the powerful and spurning (sometimes jailing or killing) the beautiful woman who has tried to seduce him. The hard-boiled detective, who may long for love and success, for a place in society, is finally driven to stand alone, resisting the blandishments of society, to pursue a lonely crusade for justice.[19]

While the detectives and the "superheroes" so popular in films share their strength, determination, and violence with their classic predecessors, the hero as a lonely outsider is obviously far different from the hero who reigns as a beloved king. They both, however, follow the same relentless logic of the ego, and its demand for power and control. In the ancient myths, the bearer of the heroic ego became a king ruling over lesser men, but if the hero cannot or does not wish to rule, then he must become a heroic outsider who follows his own path and never bends to the will of others.

From its very beginnings, the myth of the hero served the purposes of the emerging patriarchy, but a new vision of the hero has also emerged; this time as a woman. Female detectives have grown increasingly popular in contemporary fiction since the pioneering Mrs. Gladden in the 1860s, but it wasn't until much more recently and the emergence of such characters as Lisbeth Salander (the girl with the dragon tattoo) that these women began welding the physical violence so characteristic of the classic male hero. Female superheroes enter the comic genre in the 1940s and their violent prowess was clear from the start. The most notable of them, Wonder Woman, not only had the super-strength of the male heroes, but a host of magical weapons as well. As radically different as this new female hero may appear, she still embodies the power of the ego with its rationality, self-control, and individualism just like her male counterparts.

While we love to think of heroic power as noble and just, it can just as easily be put to other ends. *The Epic of Gilgamesh* describes its hero as a king who lords over his people like a raging bull, and in a telling story, he first meets his beloved Enkidu when he confronts Gilgamesh and tries to prevent him from raping a peasant woman on her wedding night. After Rama rescues Sita from the demon king, she must literally walk through fire to prove she has been faithful, and even that is not enough. Rama hears gossip about her that besmirches *his* reputation, and even though he knows it's false, he renounces her and throws her out.

The noble Odysseus and his men began their epic journey home by sacking the island of Ismarus, killing its men, raping its women, and claiming them as their booty. And when he finally returns to Ithaka, Odysseus engages in another orgy of brutality. He not only slaughters the suitors who plagued his wife during his absence, but also their soothsayer who claims he tried to dissuade them from their evil deeds, as well as a host of his own serving women who Odysseus felt had been too friendly to his foes. Penelope's devoted nurse describes the scene:

> [A]ll I heard was the choking groans of men cut down in blood … I found Odysseus in the thick of slaughtered corpses; there he stood and all around him, over the beaten floor, the bodies sprawled in heap, lying one on another …. How it would have thrilled your heart to see him—splattered with bloody filth, a lion with his kill![20]

Although we like to think of the conquering hero as a breed apart from the evil villain, he is the child of the same egoic structure, and in real life they are often mixed together.

It is tempting to ask when the ego seized control of the human psyche, but that puts the question too broadly. It appears that the foragers of the Paleolithic Era lived in a time of far more uroboric oneness, while the era of the Goddess began in the Neolithic Era with the transition to simple farming. Egoic consciousness became an increasingly powerful force as the first advanced agricultural civilizations took shape, was reinforced by the cultural revolution of the axial breakthrough, and reached its zenith in our industrial age. Yet all these stages exist simultaneously within our individual psyches and within every cultural era. The difference lies in the relative strength of these patterns, both within individuals and in society as a whole. Our psychological center may be set in one of these patterns or in a shifting balance among the three, and the same is true for our cultures as well.

Despite the romantic vision of the "noble savage," it seems doubtful that any group of modern homo sapiens ever existed in complete uroboric unity with their environment. No matter how primitive their technology, no matter how isolated they may have been from outsiders, ethnographers have never found a society whose members had no egos. The people in all known cultures have a language and personal names. They feel pride when they fulfill the expectations of their group and shame when they do not. Although it may differ from our own, they all have a sense of right and wrong. They adorn themselves with clothes and ornaments, and some are given more prestige and respect than others. Again and again, ethnographers remark on how similar the "primitive" people they studied seem to be to themselves.

On the other hand, ethnographers have also found that traditional peoples are far more identified with family, tribe, and the natural world than those from individualistic industrial societies. When, for example, ethnographers ask respondents questions like "What happens when you die?", they often get a kind of puzzled response. They can usually come up with some kind of answer, but it is often clear that they don't really think about such things very much. Their tribe and the world around them continue, and that is their immortality. In traditional societies, the center of gravity rests with the goddess not the hero.

Even in the simplest foraging societies, however, some people have a more developed ego than others. Although the early shamans are sometimes cast as the harbingers of a higher level of spiritual development, their most defining trait may well be their sense of themselves as special individuals set apart from others by their unique powers. Shamans were highly respected by their peers, but they were also feared—especially when they delved into sorcery and witchcraft—and I think it follows that they were set apart from their fellows in a way that must have required a stronger sense of self. The shaman ethnographers encountered in cultures around the world often showed pride in their special powers and a sense of superiority toward those who lacked them. Although it's unclear if they had the same kind of ego-dominated personality that characterizes our modern age, the heroes of the great myths we studied certainly did.

At first, this kind of ego-dominated personality was probably limited to a small elite—kings, priests, lords, warriors, and perhaps the occasional brigand. A less violent kind of egoism also spread among the merchants whose livelihood depended on rational calculation and self-control. Yet most people in agricultural societies continued to live in the unreflective embrace of their kin, their tribe, and their environment. In times of natural disaster, war, or other disruptions, their egos undoubtedly pushed themselves to the fore, only to soften again when things settled down.

The beginnings of modern, ego-dominated society are to be found much later in the Western European countries where the Industrial Revolution first began. The Protestant Reformation, and most especially the emergence of the Puritans, not only changed the religious landscape in Western Europe but the psychological one as well. In addition to their thorough disenchantment of their cultural world, the Puritan faiths demanded a radical, ego-dominated self-control. Singing, dancing, unnecessary luxury, fine clothes, idle chatter, and even sex for anything but reproduction were sure signs that you were among the damned, destined for eternal torment. Faithful Puritans lived in constant fear that if their self-control ever weakened, they would succumb to the satanic power of their instinctual nature. The Puritans never succeeded in displacing all their religious competitors, but their radical form of ego dominance came to prevail among the merchant classes of Northern Europe, and they in turn laid the foundations for the Industrial Revolution that was to send the traditional order crashing to the ground and remake the world.

As the Industrial Revolution progressed, people poured into cities leaving their traditional lives behind, and in the process their psychological moorings came undone as well. In a peasant village, your identity was simply given. Everybody knew you from the time you were born until you died. Your family, your gender, your occupation, who you could marry, and your place in the world were handed to you, and in most cases, they were met with unreflective acceptance. In the post-industrial world, however, we've been ripped from the arms of that maternal embrace and presented with virtually endless choices. No one hands us an identity, we have to construct it for ourselves. That can be thrilling, but terrifying as well. Again and again, we are tormented by questions like "Who am I?", "How do I fit into the world?", "Should I get married?", "What career should I pursue?", "Should I have children?", "Am I a worthwhile person?"—questions only the ego can answer.

The Awakened Mind

There's no doubt our culture idealizes the heroic ego and its embodiment in the virile male who, because of his unbounded strength, cunning, and determination, accomplishes what lesser men cannot, and in one way or another rules over them and the women who admire him. We see ego strength as so essential to the mental health of women and men that the development of the ego is often held to be the last and highest stage of psychological growth. But if that is so, why is our society crumbling and its people so desperately unhappy? The only solution traditional psychology has to offer is more of the same—building an even stronger ego. Even Carl Jung, whose spiritual insight ran far deeper than his materialistic colleagues, still saw the goal of psychological growth as one of "individuation"—the process of psychological integration in which our archetypical inheritance and our personal experience are merged together into a holistic sense of self. This is certainly an admirable goal, but it only goes so far. As in most Western psychology, his goal was a broader, healthier, and more secure sense of self, not a fundamental transformation. As long as our personality is still dominated by the ego, as long as we are hopelessly enmeshed in the drama of the self, the fundamental problem remains unchanged.

It can be hard to see our way forward from this age of egoism, but the path is there if we search for it. Ken Wilber argues that at every stage in the evolution of consciousness, there are a few exceptionally developed individuals who are harbingers of things to come, and while the attempt to confine our development to a few discrete stages inevitably leads to distortions, there is still a grain of truth in what he says. Among our most ancient ancestors, it had to have been a relatively small number of people who first developed a reflective self-awareness, and they must certainly have stood out from their fellows who still slumbered in the uroboric depths.

Among later tribal people, it was their shamans who were most likely to have expanded that modicum of self-awareness into a more highly developed ego structure. Once we enter the era of written language, we can look for actual historical individuals who were the harbingers of change. Of course, there is only so much we can know about the subjective experience of any historical figures, but we do know what they said, and on that basis there is little doubt that among all the great axial sages it is India's Siddhartha Gautama who stands out not only as the one who was the first to recognize the suffering inherent in the new ego-dominated psyche, but who made it the center of his teachings. Again and again, he told anyone who would listen that our clinging to the self-concept that we create is the fundamental cause of our suffering, and just as much as his teachings, the life he lived pointed the way to a freedom beyond the confines of the ego.

Some take that to mean that we should annihilate the ego and return to our original uroboric bliss, but there's no way for us to return to the womb, and even if we could that would deny more than a hundred thousand years of human evolution. Wilber argues that each stage in the growth of human consciousness requires not that we destroy its predecessor, but that we integrate it into a higher level of awareness. Hegel's famous three-part dialectic of thesis, antithesis, and synthesis illuminates this point. The origin or "thesis" of our psyche is the uroboric world of nature, instinct, and unreflective awareness. The "antithesis" is the ego-dominated world of individualism and rational self-control, and the "synthesis" combines them both into the transpersonal awareness of the awakened mind.

This new synthesis is beyond all duality such as the distinction between female and male, but it is nonetheless the power of the awakened feminine that leads us to that breakthrough. As Neumann takes pains to point out, the deepest layers of the psyche on which all the others depend are always matriarchal, regardless of individual circumstances. Even at the height of the heroic ego's power, the goddess's world of nature, instinct, and belonging that the hero struggles to repress still forms the foundation of the psyche, and it is in these depths that the awakening to a higher level of consciousness is born.

As a European psychologist writing in the middle of the twentieth century, Erich Neumann never seems to have plumbed the depths of Indian philosophy, but his almost instinctive understanding of our great symbols is unsurpassed. At the end of his encyclopedic work on the archetype of the Great Mother, he turned to Tara as the symbol of the highest development of the feminine principle, even though he doesn't seem to have understood the profound difference between a Buddha like Tara and the goddesses whose mythology he was exploring. The last of the hundreds of images in his book is a photo of a wonderful statue of the Noble Tara. At its base is the great tortoise, a primal mythological symbol of the material world of earth and water. The tortoise supports a tree of life that has antagonistic dragons coiling up its sides—the conflicting opposites of dualistic thought. And at the crown of the tree of life sits a lotus seat upon which is the roaring lion of the masculine spirit with his flowing mane. Above this rises the Noble Tara enthroned on her lotus seat and surrounded by a halo of the spirit—the essence of the awakened feminine (see Figure 6.4). As Neumann put it:

> The Archetypal Feminine in man unfolds like mankind itself. At the beginning stands the primeval goddess, resting in the materiality of her elementary character, knowing nothing but the secret of the womb; at the end is Tara, in her left hand the opening lotus blossom of psychic flowering, her right hand held out toward the world in a gesture of giving. Her eyes are half closed and in her meditation she turns toward the outward as well as the inner world; an eternal image of the redeeming female spirit.[21]

The awakened feminine that Neumann evokes is rooted in our body and its natural connection to the world yet reaches out with love and the spirit of redemption. In her symbolic manifestation as a female buddha, Tara makes no effort to repress the raw energy of our emotions, but she also rejoices in the clarity and power of the great heroic ego and of the intellect that allows us to see the consequences of our actions and ascend to the heights of rational understanding. Yet at the same time, she transcends them both as she transcends the division between female and male. Resting in the luminous emptiness that is our true nature, she sees our instinctive depths and the needs of our fragile ego as integral parts of the infinite web of existence that links us all together.

Figure 6.4 *Tara on the Tree of Life. Original drawing by Laura Petrucha Liss.*

The boundless state of awakening that Tara represents may appear to be completely selfless and complete, and perhaps for a cosmic buddha such as Tara that is true, but what about us ordinary humans? From a practical psychological perspective, to be completely without a sense of self is akin to some kind of psychosis—one would literally not know one's hand from the doorknob it grasped. The difference between one who manifests this wisdom and the rest of us is not that she has no self, but that she doesn't cling to it. She sees herself, her life story, and all her human connections as integral parts of the interdependent web of being. The greed, selfishness, and fear so basic to the normal ego structure still arise, but they have no more purchase than clouds floating in the vast open sky. She acts for the benefit of beings, because she immediately recognizes that any harm she might do to another, she does to herself as well; just as she knows that the loving compassion she beams out to the world will return back to her a thousandfold.

This ideal of the awakened wisdom beyond all duality is, of course, just that—an ideal. It is what Weber called an *ideal type* that we can use as a point of comparison for what we find in the real world. Some people come far closer to its full actualization than others, but the number of people who fully realize Tara's wisdom is extremely small—in much the way, the real-life heroes whose praises we sing always have their shortcomings as well. The critical question is not how to attain perfection, but how we can be midwife to the great psychological transformation to which Tara points.

Sources

The idea that the evolution of human consciousness is not just a product of a series of random accidents, but is actually going somewhere in some kind of recognizable progression is found among contemporary thinkers from many different traditions including Aurobindo, *The Devine Life* (Twin Lakes, WI: Lotus Press, 1990) and Teilhard de Chardin (*The Future of Man*, New York: Harper, 1964). The germ of this chapter comes from Erich Nuemann's wonderful book, *The History and Origins of Consciousness* (Princeton, NJ: Princeton University Press, 1954). Ken Wilber's *Up From Eden: A Transpersonal View of Human Evolution* (Boulder, CO: Shambhala Publications 1983) was very influenced by Neumann, but it takes a much broader view of the evolution of consciousness and integrates the insights of Indian thought right from the start. Joseph Campbell's focus is more on the mythology itself rather than the evolution of consciousness, but he also provides many valuable insights. I especially liked his *Goddesses: Mysteries of the Feminine Divine* (Novato, CA: New World Library, 2013).

For *The Epic of Gilgamesh,* I relied most heavily on the translation by Maureen Gallery Kovacs and for *The Odyssey,* I used the translation by Robert Fagles (New York: Penguin Books, 1996). *Beowulf: A New Verse Translation* by Seamus Heaney (New York: W.W. Norton, 2000) was my primary source for that great myth.

Robert Bellah et al., *Habits of the Heart: Individualism and Commitment in American Life* (New York: Harper & Row, 1985) has a good treatment of contemporary heroes and their relationship to the culture of individualism. Maria Tatar's *The Heroine with 1,001 Faces* (New York: Liveright, 2021) explores the many faces of the female hero in counterpoint to Campbell's famous work, *The Hero with a Thousand Faces* (Princeton, NJ: Princeton University Press, 1949). See the discussion of sources at the end of the last chapter for references to some valuable works on Tara.

7

Becoming Tara

At times it seemed that the harder I searched for Tara, the more she slipped from view. Was she the historical product of the religious currents in medieval India? A goddess? A Buddha? An archetypal symbol? The next stage in the evolution of human consciousness? The answer to all these questions is in some ways yes, but also no. Her mystery is that she lies beyond our rational mind, and try as we will, she will not be confined by our conceptual categories. Yet even though we cannot really *know* Tara with our rational calculations, we can *become* her. Just as our ancient ancestors merged with the powerful beings in song and dance, there are powerful meditation techniques that can help us access Tara's enlightened wisdom and, in the process, activate our own awakening and perhaps open new pathways into the future.

The growth of ego-consciousness seems to have happened all on its own. No one set out to develop an ego-dominated personality, it was one of many possible responses that arose in reaction to an ever-changing environment. The breakthrough to the transpersonal realm of the awakened feminine, on the other hand, usually requires intentional effort. Ironically, it seems that the same ego-controlled mind we seek to tame with our meditation can also show us the path to its own transcendence. Yet perhaps that is not really so surprising, since that ego-dominated rationality has proven to be among the most transformative forces our world has ever known. The critical question is: Do we continue to allow its intoxicating power to be an end in itself, or do we put it to a higher purpose? In the final analysis, we must transcend our egoic mind to realize Tara's wisdom, but if we avoid confusing the map rational understanding creates with the vast unbounded realm it charts, it can be an invaluable guide along the way, pointing to the awakening that lies beyond its reach.

Mindfulness

The "spiritual technology" of meditation has been shaped by thousands of years of trial and error. There are now countless techniques from a rainbow of different traditions available to seekers on the spiritual path, but it is what is known as "mindfulness" that has come to define meditation in the popular imagination. The origins of the term trace back to a nineteenth-century translation of a Pali word, *sati,* which means "memory" or "recollection." Throughout the Pali Canon, the Buddha used the word *sati* to refer to the recollection of the principles of his teachings as well as to a state in which one remembers to pay attention to one's body and mind. So mindfulness was both a type of meditation and an ongoing mental process. As Buddhism gained influence in the West, great teachers such as Thich Nhat Hanh brought mindfulness practice with them. But it soon leapt beyond the Buddhist community with its emphasis on spiritual realization into psychotherapy, pain management, programs for coping with life's distress, and even pop culture. Mindfulness practice is now taught in hospitals, corporate boardrooms, community workshops, and even in the military for everything from stress reduction to maximizing individual performance. As might be expected, as mindfulness practice spread more and more broadly, its definition expanded as well. These days mindfulness is used to refer to almost any effort to be aware of what is going on in the present moment, as well as a wide variety of meditation techniques that involve a calm, steady awareness of mind and body.

Mindfulness of breathing is in all likelihood the most commonly practiced type of meditation in the world today. Along with practices that focus on other objects such as sensations, emotions, or thoughts, mindfulness of breathing is considered by some to be the foundation upon which all other meditation techniques are based. The instructions are straightforward. You merely focus your attention unwaveringly on the in-breath and the out-breath. When your attention wanders, you bring it back to the breath—over and over again. For all its simplicity, this practice can be profound. As concentration deepens, states of joy and equanimity may spontaneously arise as may the residues of old traumas and unresolved psychological issues that demand attention.

Sitting still and just allowing our mind to settle into peaceful serenity is itself a kind of subversive act in this world of consumer capitalism that feeds on agitation and distraction. Yet contemporary mindfulness practice has its pitfalls. Its close bonds with psychotherapy mean that for many, the goal is more to build a healthier, happier ego than to transcend it. And more serious practitioners who cultivate deep states of meditative equipoise can fall into a different trap. Since fiery emotions can disrupt that equanimity, some see them as obstructions that block the way to ultimate realization. Even if they are able to loosen the grip of their egoic consciousness, their efforts to uproot or suppress their passions can lead to a tranquil detachment that is a form of denial rather than transcendence—a kind of shutting down that fails to engage with the world and the fiery dance of life.

Calling on Tara

The tantras offer a different kind of meditative path. Rather than slowly prying off the ego's grip on the psyche by using its own powers of self-discipline and rational inquiry, the tantras are a kind of end-run around the ego. Tantric practice puts the powers of imagination to work to reach the deepest levels of the subconscious mind in order to break through the obstacles that block the path to psychic transformation. As we have seen, the most distinctive characteristic of tantric practice is its use of visualizations and mantras to invoke a variety of enlightened beings known in Tibetan as *yidams*. Each of these enlightened beings appears resplendent with complex symbolism that involves everything from their color and apparel to the position of their hands (of which there may be dozens). Volumes have been written about the meaning of these symbols, but all that is beside the point. The *yidams* speak to us in the mysterious language of the unconscious world that evolved long before the rational mind of the ego. That language of myth, metaphor, and magical thinking is the realm of the primal feminine, and it speaks to a far more highly developed state as well.

Each *yidam* has its own meaning and power, but it is Tara who is most closely linked to the power of the awakened feminine. As a fully awakened Buddha, she offers an alternative to the unreflective domination of the instinctive realm of the passions, as well as to the toxic blend of ego and aggression that is choking the modern world. I can testify that even her simplest practices can have profound consequences, and at its highest level Tara practice opens the way to the transpersonal realm.

In the Buddhist tradition, most sessions of Tara practice begin by "taking refuge" in the "Three Jewels"—Buddha, Dharma (the teachings), and Sangha (community)—and firmly setting one's aspirations. Of course, those from other traditions don't take

Buddhist refuges, but it is extremely helpful to reflect on why we are doing the practice and what we hope to achieve, before we begin. For most people, the honest answer is that they are seeking to live a happier and more fulfilled life, and that is certainly a worthwhile goal that should not be belittled, but there is a higher motivation as well—not just to work for one's own benefit, but for the welfare and happiness of all beings everywhere and the whole world. That may seem an impossibly lofty aspiration, yet it's surprisingly easy to generate that kind of compassionate motivation. All you have to do is take a clear look at this world we live in with all its suffering and desperation, and from there the desire to help soothe all that pain springs up as naturally as day from night.

Once your aspirations are fixed, there are many different Tara practices to pursue. To countless people in Tibet and the Himalayan region, Tara is a friend, protector, and guide, and she is honored in rituals, songs, and celebrations. As Stephan Beyer writes: "[T]he most impressive aspect of these [Tara] rituals is the true devotion with which the Tibetans approach the goddess: she guards and protects her people, they say, from the cradle to beyond the grave, and her devotees cry out to her in their distress and share with her their joys"[1]—rather like the devotees of Isis or Mother Mary. Most people don't attempt to *merge* with Tara or achieve the kind of personal transformation that implies. Rather, whether individually or in groups led by a lama, they call out for her protection and love, often reciting her mantra, her 108 names, or a list of praises for her twenty-one traditionally recognized forms. Monastics and other full-time practitioners are far more likely to engage in lengthy Tara practices, but the exact ones they do are often kept secret, and there are significant variations depending on one's teacher and lineage, so I won't attempt to summarize them here.

Today, Tara practice has spread far beyond Tibetan culture and Tibetan Buddhist traditions, so I want to focus on the practices that have shown the most resonance in the wider world. Given the narrow patriarchal orientation of so much traditional religion, including Buddhism itself, it is not surprising that many people feel an immediate connection to the awakened feminine presence Tara embodies after nothing more than an accidental encounter with a sculpture, painting, or an image online. With time that initial connection will mature and deepen if it is cultivated with sincere meditative practice.

Tara has as many forms as there are people who envision her, but the most common entry into Tara practice is through a Green Tara who has a more-or-less normal-looking body—two eyes, two arms, and no menacing teeth—albeit one that is insubstantial and incomparably beautiful. Only her green skin marks her off as something completely outside our everyday experience.

After settling into an upright posture and setting your aspirations, you may simply visualize Green Tara in front of you, manifesting all her radiant beauty, and perhaps calling on her for guidance. Most practices, however, unfold in a series of steps like a story, and some of the visualizations can be complex, so support from a text or personal instructions from a teacher can be important, especially at the beginning.

Many texts advise the meditator to begin their visualization by bringing to mind a beautiful lotus flower with Tara's "seed syllable," the Tibetan letter *Tam,* or a ball or blue-green light resting in the middle. Once this image is stable and clear, she begins reciting Tara's Sanskrit mantra, O*ṃ Tāre Tuttāre Ture Svāhā*, over and over again. The important thing is not the meaning of the phrase but the energy it generates and the way it brings her presence to mind.

The next step is dramatic, for the power of the mantra instantly transforms the seed syllable into a radiant image of Green Tara resting on that same lotus. The descriptions of Green Tara that help meditators generate their visualizations vary from text to text and are usually rich with symbolism that may or may not resonate with people from other cultures. Her radiant beauty, beatific smile, transcendent peace, and awesome power are universally apparent, but the symbolism of her hand gestures (*mudras*), the colors of her jewels, or of the ritual implements she sometimes holds are less obvious. However you envision her, the important thing is to feel her presence and the awesome power of the primal energy she embodies. Once you have developed enough concentration to generate a stable image of Tara, you may wish to ask for her blessings, perhaps visualized as a flow of glowing nectar or rays of light that emanate from Tara's body and flow into you. Imagine yourself being bathed in the primal energy of Tara's love, and that all your fears, selfish desires, and obstructions are being washed away. Finally, you can dissolve the visualization and just rest in open awareness.

This relatively simple practice has many benefits, some obvious and some more subtle and harder to put into words. Like the mindfulness of breathing, this is a concentration practice that helps focus the mind and reduce mental chatter, and as your concentration deepens so does the feeling of peace and equanimity. However, because the focus of concentration is not on a neutral object like the breath, but on a powerful symbol of the primordial wisdom of the enlightened mind, as your concentration deepens, you might also feel a growing connection with something that is both outside yourself and a part of your deepest true nature. The energy visualized to be flowing from Tara can also have a powerful effect, soothing trauma and breaking through mental obstructions.

Becoming Tara

Once the visualization and the sense of Tara's presence are stabilized, a process that can take some time, there is a further step—from envisioning Tara to *becoming* her. Technically, it's no more difficult to visualize yourself as Tara than it is to visualize her in the sky in front of you. Psychologically, however, it's a different matter. Our egoic mind is built upon a vast network of beliefs about who we are and who we're not, and though we may think of our ego as filled with self-aggrandizement, it's just as much a product or our fears and perceived inadequacies. The "rational" ego ruminates endlessly about our failures and shortcomings. It usually has no doubt that we are not an enlightened being full of love and surpassing wisdom, and of course, that conviction traps us in our limited sense of self. By imagining ourselves as an enlightened being with all of her wisdom and power, we are freed from the self-limiting thoughts that block our progress—that inner voice of the ego that tells us we are not good enough, not strong enough, not wise enough, that the spiritual journey is a hopeless quest intended only for people far superior to us. A different kind of problem may arise for men who feel uncomfortable imagining themselves as a *female* buddha. Yet as common as that may be, many men also report a tremendous feeling of freedom when they are finally able to break through the rigid confines of their gender identification.

Imagining ourselves as Tara begins as nothing more than that—*imagination*—but as the weeks and months go by, we gradually gain the confidence that in our deepest true nature, we actually are a divine manifestation of awakened wisdom. This is what Tibetans call *vajra pride*, and it is essential to break through our self-limiting ideas. Just as a softball pitcher can actually improve her performance by imagining herself throwing the ball over and over again, imagining ourselves as an awakened being helps clear the path to that awakening.

After we set out to visualize ourselves as Tara, one further question remains: Are we to be one Tara or many? Some practices, such as the one we described above, focus on a single image of Tara who represents all the vast protean qualities of the awakened feminine. In the Appendix, there is a simple version of a traditional Green Tara practice that I love. It contains all the key elements we just described and some beautiful flourishes as well. In that practice, after stabilizing the visualization and receiving Tara's love and blessings, the meditator asks Tara to merge with them. Tara agrees, melts into light, and enters into you. You dissolve, and reappear with a shimmering body made of pure light and energy that is insubstantial and luminous. Tara merges with your mind as well, and you experience Tara's pure awakened awareness—vast emptiness suffused with love. Reciting the mantra and abiding in this enlightened state, you cultivate the conviction that you are indeed the noble Tara. At the conclusion of the practice, you slowly dissolve the visualization until there is nothing left but a blazing blue-green *Tam* or ball of light in your heart. The Tam gets smaller and smaller until it too vanishes, and then you simply rest in the true nature of your mind without contrivance or manipulation.

Even this brief description of the practice conveys some of its raw power, but there is another popular approach that refracts the awakened feminine into its component parts, each of which appears as a different form of Tara. Many of these practices are based on the traditional formulation of the twenty-one Taras. Some involve visualizations of the different Taras to which one recites various praises appropriate to her unique characteristics and then calls upon her for protection and guidance. In others, you become each of the twenty-one different Taras in turn and thereby actualize the various different qualities each embodies.

Even a simplified practice of the twenty-one Taras tends to be long and involved, and we can't reproduce an entire practice here. Instead, let's take just one of the twenty-one Taras to see how the practice is done. Tara number seven, "Tara Who Crushes Adversaries," is interesting because she seems so different from Tara's beautiful and loving forms that we've become familiar with. Zasep Tulku Rinpoche translates the traditional description of the Tara used in this practice as follows:

> From the sphere of emptiness on a yellow lotus, and a sun seat appears a black TU syllable. The TU completely transforms into me as Venerable Tara Who Crushes Adversaries. My body is black in colour with one face and four arms. My first right hand holds a Dharma wheel, and the second holds a sword. My first left hand holds a lotus on which rests a *vajra*, and the second is making a threatening mudra. I have a wrathful expression and am standing in a heroic posture; my right leg is bent and my left out-stretched. I wear jewelled ornaments on my crown. I wear armlets, bracelets and anklets. I also wear meditation threads and beautiful snakes as ornaments. I am surrounded by a blazing wisdom fire. A white OM marks my crown, a red AH my throat and a blue HUM my heart.[2]

Why would anyone want to visualize themselves as such a wrathful spirit? The answer is that the power of the awakened mind manifests in whatever form is needed, whether beautiful or frightening. Tara has all human emotions, not just sweetness and light, but wrath and fiery sensuality. While this Tara may appear to be frightening, she always uses her power for the benefit of others, crushing obstacles to liberation, negative forces, and even demons. In personal terms, she cuts off relationships that need to end and subdues those who would harm others.

As you work through the visualizations of the various Taras, you learn to embody all their enlightened qualities and emotions so that they can manifest whenever they are needed. Ten-armed Golden Tara embodies the six perfections—generosity, moral discipline, patience, perseverance, concentration, and wisdom. Four-armed Yellow Tara grants supreme spiritual power. Four-armed Red Tara dispels all suffering. Six-armed yellow Tara grants prosperity and brings about auspicious circumstances.

Lama Tsultrim Allione presents a simpler practice that seems particularly suited to contemporary times.[3] It utilizes five "wisdom dakinis" (which can be seen as forms of Tara) as primal manifestations of the awakened feminine. One begins by imagining a mandala with "White Buddha Dakini" in the center, symbolizing space, open awareness, and the wisdom of emptiness. In front of her is blue/black "Vajra Dakini," embodying water and the wisdom of mirror-like awareness. To her right is yellow "Ratna Dakini," representing earth and the wisdom of equanimity. Behind her is red "Padma Dakini," the element of fire and symbol of discriminating awareness. And to the left is green "Karma Dakini," representing wind and the wisdom of all-accomplishing activity.

After bringing the entire mandala to mind, you visualize yourself as each of the five dakinis, one after the other, bringing to mind the obstructed patterns associated with each one (delusion and depression, anger, pride, selfish desire, and envy), and vanquishing each in turn. At the end, you imagine all the dakinis together and recognize that they are all manifestations of your own true nature. You are the whole mandala. As in all other practices, you conclude by dissolving the visualization and resting in open awareness.

Before closing, we need to consider the energy yogas. Although less widely known than the meditations described above, they are among the fastest and most powerful of any meditation techniques, but the most dangerous as well. They work directly with the primal energy of life, and it is easy to lose control of the forces you invoke. If not properly done, they can result in agitation and insomnia, and vulnerable individuals may even suffer serious psychological disturbances. Moreover, like the practices that cultivate peace and tranquility, they can deteriorate into nothing more than the pursuit of blissful mental states which by their very nature are impermanent. For most people who experiment with them, however, the main problem is that they don't work without some facility with visualization practice and strong meditative concentration. The energy yogas have a unique power, but it is unwise to attempt to practice them without the guidance of an experienced teacher you trust.

The foundational practice for these yogas is known as *chandali* (Sanskrit) or *tummo* (Tibetan)—literally the "fierce goddess," and it is closely related to the Hindu practice of *kundalini* yoga. Although there are a variety of ways to practice the fierce goddess, the basic idea is the same. Practitioners use special visualizations and breathing techniques which I will not go into here to focus their *shakti*—the fiery female energy—in the *chakra* (energy center) below the navel. As the energy intensifies, it becomes hotter and hotter, and bursts into raging flames that begin shooting up the central channel that runs just in front of the spine. When the flames reach the crown *chakra* at the top of the head, they begin to melt the white drop of male energy that resides there, which begins to drip slowly down the central channel producing waves of ecstasy as it descends. When the drops reach the lower center, they feed the fire and it surges upward ever more strongly, and this in turn increases the downward flow of the white energy until the meditator is consumed in a continuous cycle of bliss. In the final stage, the meditator lets their blissful awareness expand into the vast emptiness that lies at the root of all things in what is known as the union of bliss and emptiness, or if you will, the union of the female and the male.

It is easy to see the echoes of the spirituality of our primal ancestors in these tantric practices, and some would even call them primitive or superstitious, but that is a profound misunderstanding. Tantric visualization practices do mark a return to the ancient roots of our primal spirituality but at a far more sophisticated level, and the same is true of the energy yogas. When a Tibetan villager calls on Tara for her protection and guidance, she points in an entirely different direction than the powerful beings of the enchanted garden or the ancient gods. Completely lacking their capriciousness or any hint of selfish motivation, she guides us unfailingly toward universal compassion and love. Merging with her takes us even farther, for it is to go beyond our primal connection to nature or the animal world and realize the boundless awareness of the enlightened mind. The ecstasy of the trance dances, the hypnotic drumming and chants, and potent mind-alternating drugs all have immense power that can be unstable and even dangerous. As we saw among the !Kung, for example, many people literally go crazy when they first enter the trance state and primal energy surges uncontrollably through their body. When properly performed with the guidance of a good teacher, the tantric energy yogas allow the practitioner to cultivate that same ecstatic bliss, but also to direct its flow and control its power, and perhaps more importantly, to use that power to burn away the obstacles to the realization of pure enlightened wisdom.

***

At the beginning, it is helpful to experiment with different approaches to meditation to see how they work, but if you do decide that Tara practice is the right path for you, I recommend you start with something simple and build up from there. It is important to remember that no practice is inherently better than another. They can all lead to deep realizations and a fundamental rebalancing of psychic energy, but at the same time, none of them is foolproof. Everyone is different, and a technique may have revelatory power at one point in your life but seem to be nothing but a dead end at another. The important thing is just to begin the journey and then see it through to the end, and wherever that is, Tara surely awaits.

Sources

The work that set off the "mindfulness revolution" is John Kabat-Zinn's *Full Catastrophe Living* (Delta Trade Paperbacks, 1991). In it, he sets forth the principles of his mindfulness-based stress reduction program that has become so popular around the world. Its focus on the therapeutic goal of stress reduction sets it apart from the more traditional emphasis on spiritual liberation, but it uses many of the same techniques found in traditional Buddhist meditation. For a more explicitly Buddhist approach to mindfulness, see Thich Nhat Hanh's *The Sutra on the Full Awareness of Breathing*, (Berkeley: Parallax Press, 1988), and Joseph Goldstein's *Mindfulness: A Practical Guide to Awakening* (Boulder, CO: Sounds True, 2013).

My favorite introduction to Tara practice is Lama Pladen Drolma's "Envisioning Tara" which appeared as chapter 6 in my previous book, *The Buddha's Dream of Liberation* (Somerville, MA: Wisdom Publications, 2017). There are a variety of works on the practice of the twenty-one Taras. Martin Willson's *In Praise of Tara: Songs to the Saviouress*, (London: Wisdom Publications, 1986) contains translations of original Sanskrit texts and a commentary from the Suryagupta tradition. Thubten Chodron, *How to Free Your Mind: The Practice of Tara the Liberator* (Boston: Snow Lion, 2005) gives instructions for a practice that involves visualizing and praising the twenty-one Taras, but without actually becoming them. Zasep Tulku Rinpoche's practice instructions in *Tara in the Palm of Your Hand: A Guide to the Practice of the Twenty-One Taras* (Nelson, BC: Wind Horse Press, 2013) include the self-visualization as Tara as does Chandra Easton's *Embodying Tara: Twenty-One Manifestations to Awaken Your Innate Wisdom* (Boulder, CO: Shambhala, 2023). Rachael Wooten gives the practice of the twenty-one Taras a Jungian slant in *Tara: The*

Liberating Power of the Female Buddha, (Boulder, CO: Sounds True, 2020). *Skillful Grace: Tara Practice for Our Times* by Tulku Urgyen Rinpoche and Trulshik Adeu Rinpoche (Hong Kong: Rangjung Yeshe Publications, 2007) gives instructions for a very comprehensive Green Tara practice whose many stages cover everything from the most basic preliminaries to the highest energy yogas.

The dakini practices mentioned in this chapter come from Lama Tsultrim Allione, *Wisdom Rising: Journey into the Mandala of the Empowered Feminine* (New York: Simon & Schuster, 2018). Lama Thubten Yeshe's *The Bliss of Inner Fire: Heart Practice of the Six Yogas of Naropa* (Somerville, MA: Wisdom Publications, 1998) is the best introduction I have found to the practice of the fierce goddess. Despite the title, his focus is only on first of the six yogas—what is called *tummo* in Tibetan. For a more complete treatment of the six yogas see Ian Baker, *Tibetan Yoga: Principles and Practices* (Rochester, VT: Inner Traditions, 2019).

Afterword
The Way Forward

There's no doubt that the heroic ego with its rationality and self-control has transformed the world. We can fly through the air, banish dread diseases, create life from chains of genetic code, pour out undreamed-of riches, and wreak fiery destruction like vengeful gods. Yet the happiness these wonders promised slips through our fingers as the carnage piles higher and higher. The world grows hotter, the seas keep rising, we fill the land with toxins, and up to 150 species are driven to extinction *every day*. The tenor of our times is not one of contentment, but anger and despair. There's a growing sense this era may be coming to an end, but the path ahead remains shrouded in darkness.

It is easy to imagine a new world sprouting up in the remains of the old, one based on sharing, mutual support, stewardship of the natural world, and the equality of all beings; but how can that vision possibly be achieved? Even humankind's most revolutionary attempts to reshape the world have only created new problems as formidable as the old. Time and again, impassioned leaders who condemned the corruption, arrogance, and self-dealing of the old regimes they challenged succumb to the same temptations when they reach power. Idealistic visions are fine, but they are doomed to failure when we are still driven by our egoic greed.

To me at least, it's clear that the foundation for a new world must be laid within, and that Tara points the way. The heroic ego has given us unprecedented dominion over our natural competitors, but its assault on the primal goddess of our instinctual nature has left us rigid, unbalanced, and bubbling with repressed desires. Tara is the rebirth of the goddess. Not as the primal deity who would conquer the ego and absorb it back into her womb, but as something entirely new. Tara embodies the primal feminine energy of life, yet she wields the power of the rational mind with sublime skill, and she holds them both in the boundless love of enlightened awareness.

Ken Wilber argues that in each age, a few great individuals embody the next level of consciousness struggling to be born. It seems, however, it is Tara who most fully manifests this new transformation of consciousness. The question is: Do we have the wisdom to see where she leads? If this sounds intriguing, there are concrete steps you can take. If you have never done Tara practice, you can begin simply by calling out to her. Find a quiet place and envision Tara in front of you with all her enlightened wisdom and power. Don't be discouraged if it takes a while. At some point, you will feel her presence, and when you do, open your heart and see what happens. If you feel some connection, you should start a regular Tara practice. Finding a teacher is great, but if you can't find someone, there are plenty of resources in books (including this one) and online to guide you. What you will need, sooner or later, is the support of "spiritual friends" who share your aspirations. Some of the greatest spiritual masters have lived solitary lives in the wilderness, but the crises of our time compel us to band together and engage with the suffering of the world. Realizing the power of the awakened feminine will mean something different to each of us, but it is in loving interaction with each other that our realization will emerge.

The Chinese character for crisis is a combination of the radicals for danger and opportunity. The dangers of our time are clear, but what of the opportunities? Just as the ego-dominated psyche spread from a relatively small elite to the masses of post-industrial society, we could be on the brink of another transition to a higher level of consciousness. The cracks in the walls of patriarchal repression grow ever wider, and as each of us evolves, new pathways open. Literacy and mass education have made the most profound teachings available to anyone who is interested, and ever-growing affluence has created the leisure time to pursue them. Of course, no one can be certain what the future holds. The worldwide disaster that seems to loom on the horizon may be unavoidable. What I do know is that whatever comes, Tara will be there to point the way forward, and it is up to us to follow her lead.

Appendix Noble Green Tara: Brief Practice

After settling the mind, say the refuge prayer, then out of emptiness, visualize that in the sky in front of you, from her seed syllable, Tam Green Tara instantly appears, sitting on a full open lotus and moon seat.

She is blue-green, the color of a mountain lake. She is arrayed in silks and jewels, symbolizing the complete integration of the six perfections and full awakening.

Radiate light from your heart to purify the phenomenal world, making offerings to the enlightened ones, and inviting Tara's actual wisdom aspect to come be present with you.

Visualize this happening by numerous small forms of Tara raining down into the visualized form uniting the two, so that the imagined aspect has become inseparable with the true wisdom aspect. Think that all your spiritual teachers' mind streams are united with her, and that she is now truly present in the sky in front of you.

She is the Mother of all the Buddhas, the essence of compassion in action. Her right foot is slightly extended; she is ready to leap to the aid of beings. Her right hand is opened out on her right knee, in the gesture of generosity. Her left hand holds the stem of a lotus flower, which is blossoming next to her left ear.

While you are repeating her mantra, **Om Tare Tu Tare Ture Svaha,** visualize that from her outstretched right hand comes a river of *amrita* (nectar), liquid light, turquoise-green in color. The river of *amrita* removes all fear, gives protection, removes obstacles and obscurations, and transmits enlightened awareness into you and all beings.

Make prayers to Tara, and receive her blessing. Then see Tara dissolve into light and dissolve as light into you. Think that your mind is inseparable with Tara's mind and with all enlightened mind. See yourself in the form of Tara, appearing as a body made of light, inseparable with emptiness, emptiness and form.

In your heart area is a blue-green *Tam*. From this seed syllable light radiates out to all beings, sending joy, compassion, loving kindness, strength, equanimity, and all qualities of enlightened mind. Keep repeating the mantra as you imagine this.

When you are done repeating the mantra, gradually dissolve the visualization until there is just a drop of turquoise-green light life in the heart area, radiating brilliantly: the essence of your true nature. This then dissolves into space, like a rainbow disappearing into the sky. Rest your mind naturally for a few minutes or longer. Dedicate the merit of the practice to all beings.

This practice text was written by Karma Palden Drolma for the use of the students at the Sukhasiddhi Foundation. For more information visit: https://www.sukhasiddhi.org/

Notes

Chapter 2: The Enchanted Garden

1 Writing this section seemed something like walking through a minefield waiting to step on one explosive anthropological disagreement or another. I have done my best to give fair consideration to all sides of these debates, but there will undoubtedly be many who disagree with my approach.

2 David Graeber & David Wengrow, *The Dawn of Everything: A New History of Humanity* (New York: Farrar, Straus and Giroux, 2021).

3 The Paleolithic Age, sometimes called the Old Stone Age, is the period of prehistory from approximately 3.3 million years ago to around 12,000 years ago, during which early humans developed the use of basic stone tools and artifacts.

4 Huston Smith, *The World's Religions* (San Francisco, CA: Harper, 1991) p. 371.

5 Colin M. Turnbull, *The Forest People* (New York: Simon & Schuster, 1961) p. 92.

6 Robert Tonkinson, *The Mardudjara Aborigines: Living the Dream in Australia's Desert* (New York: Holt, Rinehart and Winston, 1984) pp. 87–88.

7 Ellen B. Basso, *Musical View of the Universe: Kalapalo Myth and Ritual Performances* (Philadelphia: University of Pennsylvania Press, 1985) p. 253.

8 Brian Hayden, *Shamans Sorcerers and Saints: A Prehistory of Religion* (Washington, DC: Smithsonian Books, 2003) p. 88.

9 Robert N. Bellah, *Religion in Human Evolution: From the Paleolithic to the Axial Age* (Cambridge, MA: Harvard University Press, 2011) p. 148.

10 Smith, *The World's Religions*, p. 367.

11 Richard B. Lee, *The Dobe !Kung* (New York: Holt, Rinehart and Winston, 1984) p. 106.

12 Hayden, *Shamans Sorcerers and Saints*, pp. 68–69.

13 The work of Napoleon Chagnon ignited one of the most bitter and personal controversies in a field already noted for its contentiousness. The "pro" and "anti" Chagnon camps cannot even agree on the name of these people. I follow Chagnon's usage since I am quoting his work, but his opponents call them the "Yanomami."

14 Napoleon Chagnon, *Yanomano: The Fierce People* (New York: Holt, Rinehart and Winston, 1968) p. 52.

Chapter 3: The Coming of the Gods

1 Marija Gimbutas, *The Language of the Goddess* (San Francisco, CA: Harper & Row, 1989) p. 321.

2 Marija Gimbutas, *The Living Goddesses*, edited and supplemented by Miriam Robbins Dexter (Berkeley: University of California Press, 1999) p. 5.

3 Diane Wolkstein and Samuel Noah Kramer, *Inanna: Queen of Heaven and Earth* (New York: HarperCollins, 1983) p. 12.

4 Ibid. p. 71.

5 Samuel Noah Kramer, *From the Poetry of Sumer* (Berkeley: University of California Press, 1979) p. 95.

6 Thorkild Jacobsen, *The Treasures of Darkness: A History of Mesopotamian Religion* (New Haven, CT: Yale University Press, 1976) p. 137.

7 R. E. Witt, *Isis in the Graeco-Roman World* (London: Thames & Hudson, 1971) pp. 134–135.

8 *The Golden Ass of Apuleius*, trans. Robert Graves (New York: Pocket Library, 1954) pp. 238– 239.

9 Exodus 32:27–29.

10 Thomas Merton, *New Seeds of Contemplation* (Boston, MA: Shambhala, 2003) pp. 172–3. I would like to thank the Merton scholar, Robert Inchausti, for his insightful help in reviewing this short section on the Virgin Mary and suggesting this quotation.

11 Quoted in Gerda Lerner, *The Creation of Patriarchy* (Oxford: Oxford University Press, 1986) pp. 142–143.

12 Amos 3:8.

13 For a more detailed account of this revelation, see Karen Armstrong, *A History of God* (New York: Ballantine Books, 1993) pp. 137–139.

Chapter 4: The Disenchanted World

1 Wing-Tsit Chan, trans., *Tao-Te Ching* in Wing-Tsit Chan, *A Source Book in Chinese Philosophy* (Princeton, NJ: Princeton University Press, 1963) pp. 142, 168.

2 Geoffrey Samuel, *The Origins of Yoga and Tantra: Indic Religions to the Thirteenth Century* (Cambridge: Cambridge University Press, 2008) pp. 173–174.

3 While the *Upanishads*, the texts with their origins in the community of Brahmanical renunciates, expressed great mystical understanding, they say little about universal ethics. Perhaps this is because the Brahmins were the hereditary priests of the Vedic religion which told them that they sat atop of a society composed of four hierarchically ranked *varnas* (or what later came to be called castes), and they consequently bridled at the universalistic claim that members of the lowest varnas should be treated equally.

4 Lao Tzu, *The Way of Life*, trans. Witter Bynner (New York: Capricorn Books, 1944) p. 25.

5 *Dhammacakkappavattana Sutta: Setting the Wheel of Dhamma in Motion*, SN 56.11, trans, Thanissaro Bhikkhu, 1993, https://www.accesstoinsight.org/tipitaka/sn/sn56/sn56.011.than.html.

6 Max Weber, *The Protestant Ethic and the Spirit of Capitalism*, https://www.marxists.org/reference/archive/weber/protestant-ethic/ no pagination.

7 Alan Wallace and Brian Hodel, *Embracing Mind: The Common Ground of Science & Spirituality* (Boston, MA, and London: Shambhala, 2008) pp. 24–25.

Chapter 5: The Goddess Who Became a Buddha

1 Many works contains a version of this story, such as Taranatha's (1507–1634) *Golden Rosary, A History Illuminating the Origin of the Tantra of Tara,* but this rending follows the version in Khenpo Tsultrim Gyamtso Rinpoche's *Tara Terma* more closely. See *Prayer Book* (San Rafael, CA: Sukhasiddhi Foudation, 2013).

2 D. L. Snellgrove *Indo-Tibetan Buddhism: Indian Buddhists and Their Tibetan Successors* (London: Serindia, 1987) pp. 170–171.

3 Bhikkhu Nanamoli and Bhikkhu Bodhi, trans., *The Middle Length Discourses of the Buddha: A Translation of the Majjhima Nikaya* (Somerville, MA: Wisdom Publications, 1995) p. 929.

4 Ibid. p. 596.

5 Stephan Beyer, *Magic and Ritual in Tibet: The Cult of Tara* (Delhi: Motilal Banarsidass, 1973) p. 14.

6 David Kinsley, *Tantric Visions of the Divine Feminine: The Ten Mahavidyas* (Delhi: Motilal Banarsidass, 1998) p. 1.

7 Krsnananda Agamavagisa, *Brhat Tantrasdra* quoted in Kinsley, *The Goddesses' Mirror*, p. 100.

8 Some Tibeto-Burman languages do not distinguish between what we call blue and black, and in any case, blue and black symbolize the same elementary energy among Tibetan *Yidam*.

Chapter 6: The Transformation of the Psyche

1 Joseph Campbell, *Goddesses: Mysteries of the Feminine Divine* (Novato, CA: New World Library, 2013) p. 13.

2 C.G. Jung, "Forword," p. xiv in Erich Neumann, *The Origins and History of Consciousness* (Princeton, NJ: Princeton University Press, 1954).

3 See endnote 39.

4 Quoted in Neumann, *The Origins and History of Consciousness,* p. 8.

5 Ibid. pp. 10 & 11.

6 *The Way and Its Power: The Tao Te Ching and Its Place in Chinese Thought*, trans. Arthur Waley (New York: Grove Press, 1958), verse 25.

7 Neumann, *The Origins of History of Consciousness*, p. 15.

8 Joseph Campbell, *Primitive Mythology: The Masks of God, Volume I* (Novato, CA: New World Library, 1959) p. 61.

9 *Nibbana Sutta*, trans. Thanissaro Bhikkhu, footnote 2, https://www.accesstoinsight.org/tipitaka/kn/ud/ud.8.03.than.html.

10 Ken Wilber, *Up from Eden: A Transpersonal View of Human Evolution* (Boulder, CO: Shambhala Publications, 1983) p. 27.

11 *The Lao Tze (Tao-te Ching)*, Wing-Tsit Chan, trans., *A Source Book in Chinese Philosophy* (Princeton, NJ: Princeton University Press, 1963) p. 160.

12 John S. Major, *"Myth, Cosmogony, and the Origins of Chinese Science," Journal of Chinese Philosophy* (1978) pp. 1–20.

13 Quoted in https://www.britannica.com/topic/creation-myth/Types-of-cosmogonic-myths.

14 Johannes C. Andersen, *Myths and Legends of the Polynesians* (London: George G. Harrap, 1928) pp. 367–368. Quoted in Neumann, *The Origins of History of Consciousness*, pp. 102–103.

15 Louise Kaplan, *Oneness and Separateness* (New York: Simon and Schuster, 1978), quoted in Wilber, *Up from Eden*, p. 119.

16 *The Epic of Gilgamesh*, trans. E. A. Speiser, in James B. Pritchard (ed.), *Ancient Near Eastern Texts* (Princeton, NJ: Princeton University Press, 1950) p. 84.

17 *The Epic of Gilgamesh*, trans. Kovacs, p. 37.

18 Homer, *The Odyssey*, trans. Robert Fagles (New York Penguin Books 1996) pp. 252–253.

19 Robert Bellah et al., *Habits of the Heart: Individualism and Commitment in American Life* (New York: Harper & Row, 1985) p. 146.

20 Homer, *The Odyssey*, trans. Fagles, pp. 456–457.

21 Erich Neumann, *The Great Mother: An Analysis of the Archetype* (Princeton, NJ: Princeton University Press, 1955) pp. 334–335.

Chapter 7: Becoming Tara

1 Stephan Beyer, *Magic and Ritual in Tibet: The Cult of Tara* (Delhi, India: Motilal Banarsidass, 1988) p. 3.

2 Zasep Tulku Rinpoche, *Tara in the Palm of Your Hand: A Guide to the Practice of the Twenty-One Taras* (Nelson, BC: Wind Horse Press, 2013) p. 111.

3 Lama Tsultrim Allione, *Wisdom Rising: Journey into the Mandala of the Empowered Feminine* (New York: Enliven Books, 2018) pp. 251–266.

Index

About the Author

James William Coleman earned a PhD from UC Santa Barbara, specializing in the sociology of religion, and is now Professor of Sociology Emeritus at California Polytechnic State University in San Luis Obispo. He studied Buddhism intensively under Roshi Reb Anderson of the San Francisco Zen Center and later with Lama Palden Drolma in the Kagyu Shangpa lineage of Kalu Rinpoche, and considers Toni Packer to be his root teacher. He is a founding member of the White Heron Sangha, a peer-led community that welcomes practices from all Buddhist traditions, where he teaches and practices.

His numerous articles have been published in such places as the *Journal of Christian/Buddhist Studies, Buddhadharma* and the *American Journal of Sociology*. His books include *The New Buddhism: The Western Transformation of an Ancient Tradition* (2001) and *The Buddha's Dream of Liberation: Freedom, Emptiness, and Awakened Nature* (2017). He was also the editor of Roshi Reb Anderson's *The Third Turning of the Wheel: Wisdom of the Samdhinirmocana Sutra* (2012).

He lives in San Luis Obispo, California with his wife and two cats, and near his two daughters and their children. Visit jameswilliamcoleman.com